Advance praise for *Studying The Hurt Locker*

Terence McSweeney's account of *The Hurt Locker* is as punchy and pugnacious as Kathryn Bigelow's movie is immersive. A masterful dissection of a weighty and important film that, as McSweeney says, continues to resonate for good and ill with audiences and critics alike. McSweeney's analysis is tellingly crisp and all the better for its no-nonsense style and whip smart observations. The film has been described as a twenty-first-century landmark in war cinema, a description which McSweeney's fascinating portrait complicates and questions at each and every turn. A terrific achievement.

Ian Scott, Senior Lecturer in American Studies, University of Manchester

Terence McSweeney always writes with clarity, insight and nuance, and this book is no exception. His ability to analyse film by illuminating the fine layers of its contemporary contexts and implications is on full display here, and it's all organised in such a way that both scholars and students can find what they need. A great addition to the bookshelf for those studying war, film and post-9/11 politics.

Dr. Stacey Peebles, NEH Associate Professor of English and Director of Film Studies, Centre College

More than any war film since *Saving Private Ryan*, *The Hurt Locker* deserves close critical attention—as a skillful piece of filmmaking, a critically and commercially acclaimed Hollywood product, and a contribution to the debate about war as an indispensable part of American foreign politics. As the film continues to reward repeated encounters, Terence McSweeney helps us to see both its importance in its own historical moment and its continued relevance.

Steffen Hantke, author of *Monsters in the Machine: Science Fiction Film and the Militarization of America after World War II*

T0317401

STUDYING THE HURT LOCKER

Terence McSweeney

Dedication

For Ben. We'll always have Bolivia.

First published in 2019 by
Auteur, 24 Hartwell Crescent, Leighton Buzzard LU7 1NP
www.auteur.co.uk

Copyright © Auteur Publishing 2019

Designed and set by Nikki Hamlett at Cassels Design www.casselsdesign.co.uk

British Library Cataloguing-in-Publication Data
A catalogue record for this book is available from the British Library

ISBN: 978-1-911325-73-4 paperback
ISBN: 987-1-911325-74-1 ebook

Contents

Factsheet

The Hurt Locker

A Voltage Pictures presentation, in association with Grosvenor Park Media and FCEF, of a Voltage Pictures, First Light, Kingsgate Films production.

Directed by Kathryn Bigelow.

Produced by Kathryn Bigelow, Mark Boal, Nicolas Chartier, Greg Shapiro.

Screenplay by Mark Boal.

Crew -

Director of Photography, Barry Ackroyd; editors, Bob Murawski, Chris Innis; music, Marco Beltrami, Buck Sanders; music supervisor, John Bissell; production designer, Karl Juliusson; art director, David Bryan; costume designer, George Little; sound (Dolby Digital), Ray Beckett; sound designer, Paul N.J. Ottosson; stunt coordinator, Robert Young; special effects supervisor, Richard Stutsman.

Running time: 127 minutes.

Cast - Staff Sgt. William James - Jeremy Renner, Sgt. J.T. Sanborn - Anthony Mackie, Specialist Owen Eldridge - Brian Geraghty, Sgt. Matt Thompson - Guy Pearce, Contractor Team Leader - Ralph Fiennes, Col. Reed - David Morse, Connie James – Evangeline Lilly, Col. John Cambridge - Christian Camargo, 'Beckham' - Christopher Sayegh.

Budget - $15 million.

Domestic Box Office - $17 million.

International Box Office - $32.2 million.

Release Date - September 4 2008 (Venice), June 26 2009 (United States), August 28 2009 (UK).

List of Illustrations

Figure 1- The very first shots of the film are taken from the perspective of the remote-control bomb disposal robot, plunging audiences into the world of *The Hurt Locker* with no frame of spatial or temporal reference.

Figure 2- The film's visual aesthetic attempts to recreate the chaos of Baghdad in 2004 with American forces tasked with bringing order to the troubled region.

Figure 3- Sanborn (Anthony Mackie) and Thompson (Guy Pearce) in a tight two-shot with much of the frame obscured by a figure to the right later revealed to be Eldridge (Brian Geraghty)

Figure 4- One of many point of view shots the film offers taken through the rifle of an American soldier, as Sanborn scrutinises the suspicious 'the Butcher' (Omar Mario) who is shown clasping a phone.

Figure 5- A close up shot of the Butcher's eyes just before he detonates the IED which kills the genial Thompson.

Figure 6- In extreme slow-motion Thompson is caught in the explosion, an incident that is repeated several times in quick succession in a film described by Bigelow as 'reportorial' and designed to not 'impose an aesthetic'.

Figure 7- One of several close ups shot in extreme slow motion during the explosion seen in Figure 6.

Figure 8- The unnamed taxi driver on the streets of Baghdad shown via his cracked rear-view mirror, one of a myriad of dangerous and threatening Iraqis the film provides audiences with.

Figure 9- The standoff with the taxi driver accentuates James' masculine prowess and his steely poise on the battlefield.

Figure 10- James reveals the extent and the danger of the IED known as a 'daisy chain' in a shot that was also used in the film's marketing and even in some of the posters on release.

Figure 11- The threats to the EOD team seem to come from everywhere and everyone regardless of age or gender. Here outside the United Nations building Iraqis watch them from a minaret. Sanborn is surprised and suspicious when they do not wave back at an American soldier pointing a loaded gun at them.

Figure 12- James informs an impressed Colonel Reed (David Morse) that he has disconnected 873 bombs.

Figure 13- The rule-breaking James emerges from the smoke as an embodiment of the maverick masculine ideal that has filled the screens of American cinema for more than a hundred years.

Figure 14- A range of cinematic devices accentuate the power and control James has over his environment.

Figure 15- James' relationship with the young Iraqi boy Beckham (Christopher Sayegh) the "base rat" is the closest he comes to another human being in the film.

Figure 16- A dead child on a table ready to be used as a human IED by monstrous insurgents, James is convinced it is Beckham, but Sanborn and Eldridge are not.

Figure 17- James brings the dead child out of the building in a sequence symbolic of the distinction the film draws between the altruism of American heroes and the perfidy of their Iraqi insurgent counterparts.

Figure 18- The unnamed contract team leader (Ralph Fiennes) shows James and Eldridge the 'Most Wanted' playing cards and his bounty in the desert.

Figure 19- James goes AWOL in the search for Beckham's murderers, running through Baghdad alone at night in the film's most criticised sequence. The shot here is blurred because the whole scene is shot in a frenetic and destabilised fashion.

Figure 20- James finds himself not in a bomb factory as he (and perhaps we) had expected but the Iraqi domestic space where he meets the surprisingly cordial Professor Nabil (Nabil Koni) who invites him in.

Figure 21- James gazes at the aftermath of the tanker bombing as Bigelow and Boal ask audiences to take a good look at what the Iraqis do to each other.

Figure 22- The reluctant suicide bomber and "family man" on the EOD team's last day and last mission 'in country'.

Figure 23- The way the scene is shot and presented has been read by many as having a richly significant symbolic potency.

Figure 24- James is caught in the suicide bomb explosion with vivid echoes of the one which killed Thompson in the film's prologue two hours of diegetic screen time before.

Figure 25- Back in the United States, but is he really at home? James visits a supermarket and despite the array of products he finds nothing of value for him there.

Figure 26- In the film's most intimate moment, James articulates his hunger for war and the thrill which it provides him with to his infant son.

Figure 27- Coming home to Iraq? Does James smile as he returns to the conflict which defines him as a man?

Figure 28- The film's final image of James walking towards the horizon as the countdown begins again.

Introduction

> The myth of war and the drug of war wait to be tasted. The mythical
> heroes of the past loom over us. Those who can tell us the truth are
> silenced or prefer to forget. The state needs the myth, as much as it
> needs its soldiers and its machines of war, to survive.
> Chris Hedges, *War is a Force that Gives Us Meaning* (2002: 173)

Kathryn Bigelow's *The Hurt Locker* (2008) is without a doubt one of the
definitive American war films of the twenty-first century. It was the first
film from the genre to have won an Academy Award for Best Picture since
Oliver Stone's *Platoon* (1986) more than twenty years before and it received
more than a hundred different awards all over the globe throughout 2009
and into 2010. During the lead up to the 2010 Academy Awards the film
found itself pitched against the science fiction blockbuster *Avatar* (2009)
directed by Bigelow's former spouse, James Cameron, a fact that the
media devoted a considerable amount of time to discussing, especially
when both films were the recipient of exactly nine nominations apiece.
Ultimately, *The Hurt Locker* was the winner on the evening of 7 March
2010, securing six Oscars: Best Picture, Best Director, Best Original
Screenplay, Best Film Editing, Best Sound Editing and Best Sound Mixing,
with *Avatar* the winner of three (Best Art Direction, Best Cinematography
and Best Visual Effects). While on the surface, *The Hurt Locker* and *Avatar*
seem far removed from one another – one is a visceral depiction of the
day-to-day experiences of a United States Army Explosive Ordnance
Disposal unit (EOD) deployed in Iraq in 2004 and the other is a science
fiction action-adventure set in and around the fictional planet of Pandora
in the second half of the twenty-second century – on closer consideration
it is clear to see that they are both immersed in the turbulent geo-
political climate of the post-9/11 era which becomes dramatically realised
within the frames of their screens. Bigelow's film might be a direct
representation of the then still ongoing Iraq War (2003-2011), but the
interplanetary colonial narrative of *Avatar*, with its military searching for
a precious resource known as Unobtanium and lines of dialogue such
as 'Our only security lies in pre-emptive attack. We will fight terror with
terror!' was frequently read as being just as much about the '9/11 wars', as
the conflicts in Iraq and Afghanistan were memorably described by Jason
Burke in his book of the same name (2012), and was widely considered an
allegorical commentary of the conflict (see Mirrlees, 2013; Kavadlo, 2015).

The Hurt Locker is a vivid and dynamically realised film and like the most resonant examples of the genre it should be regarded as a powerful cultural artefact intrinsically connected to the times in which it was made. It was widely acclaimed on its release and as well as the numerous awards mentioned above sites like Metacritic and Rotten Tomatoes, as clumsy and unscientific barometers as they are, offer testimony to this acclaim. It achieved a ninety-four percent rating at Metacritic (which places it in the company of films like *Pulp Fiction* [1994] and *The Manchurian Candidate* [1962]) and ninety-eight percent 'fresh' on Rotten Tomatoes (a level also earned by *E.T. The Extra-Terrestrial* [1982] and *King Kong* [1933]). Reviews of the film tended to focus on a few particular areas: its authenticity, its realism, its ability to 'show the war as it really is', and its kinetic and immersive qualities. The majority read something along the lines of Kenneth Turan's in the *Los Angeles Times* who wrote that *The Hurt Locker* was 'overwhelmingly tense, overflowing with crackling verisimilitude, it's both the film about the war in Iraq that we've been waiting for and the kind of unqualified triumph that's been long expected from director Kathryn Bigelow' (2009) or David Denby's in *The New Yorker*, which suggested that it was 'a small classic of tension, bravery, and fear, which will be studied twenty years from now when people want to understand something of what happened to American soldiers in Iraq. If there are moviegoers who are exhausted by the current fashion for relentless fantasy violence, this is the convincingly blunt and forceful movie for them' (2009).

In subsequent years many have been more critical of the film. While writers frequently continue to register the skilfulness with which it was created, its impact and its cultural significance, many have increasingly explored the problematic nature of its political perspectives and the accuracy of claims like those of Kathryn Bigelow herself that the film should be understood as 'real and as authentic' (qtd. in Dawson, 2013: 145) and that it did not 'impose an aesthetic' on its subject matter (qtd. in Rubin, 2011: 268), or interrogated the assertions of writers who had suggested that it attempted a 'documentary approach to the war experience' (Trafton, 2016: 61) and even 'stripped out almost every single moment that might be judged political' (Barker, 2011: 156).

Unlike *Avatar*, which made a remarkable $2.7 billion dollars at the world-wide box office, leading to it becoming the most financially successful film of all time, *The Hurt Locker* was one of a number of films about the wars in Iraq and Afghanistan, like *In the Valley of Elah* (2007), *Stop-Loss* (2008), *Brothers* (2009) and *Green Zone* (2010), to financially underperform, often despite the presence of big name stars, to such an extent that to make a film set in Iraq or Afghanistan was considered for many years to be 'box office poison' (Everheart, 2009) and the Iraq War film itself was, according to Martin Barker, even 'a toxic genre' in his book *A 'Toxic Genre': The Iraq War Films* (2011). *The Hurt Locker* earned just $17 million at the US box office (with a world-wide total of $49 million), meaning that it is, at the time of writing, the lowest grossing film to win an Academy Award for Best Picture by quite some margin.

This book is an analysis of *The Hurt Locker*, of its stylistic and narrative devices, of its cultural impact, of its reception, of its relationship to the genre and ultimately of what it is able to tell us about a war which was officially brought to an end by President Barack Obama on the 18 December 2011, but is one which still continues to be fought onscreen in films like *American Sniper* (2014), Billy Lynn's *Long Half-Time Walk* (2016), *Sand Castle* (2017), *War Machine* (2017), *The Wall* (2017) and *12 Strong* (2018). One of this book's central contentions is that the key to the affective impact of *The Hurt Locker*, both at the time of its release and a decade later, can be located in the ambiguity with which it is constructed, by which I suggest that its director, Kathryn Bigelow, its writer, Mark Boal, its director of cinematography, Barry Ackroyd, its sound designer, Paul N.J. Ottosson and even the performances by the likes of Jeremy Renner and Anthony Mackie (both of whom won several awards for their portrayals of members of the EOD unit on rotation in Baghdad) participate in a film which is designed to invite numerous different interpretations and experiences on the part of spectators, even though it is certainly what we would consider a mainstream film. This might explain, at least in part, why reactions to it have been so diverse and not just dissimilar, as one might expect with any film, but almost paradoxical, as if *different* viewers had actually seen a *different* film. Thus, Michael Smith can describe *The Hurt Locker* as 'an apolitical film. It is neither an anti-war film nor a pro-war film. It is, simply, a great war film about courageous men working in chaotic situations, and the collateral damage that comes with the job' (2009), at the very same time as the historian Marilyn Young, the author of *The Vietnam Wars 1945-1990* (1991), argues that it should be seen as 'a video game of a movie, or war as a video game' (2009). Elizabeth Wietzman, writing for the *New York Daily News*, is able to make the rather grandiose claim that *The Hurt Locker* is 'the war movie this era needs' (2009), while at the same time John Pilger convincingly argues that 'This film offers a vicarious thrill through yet another standard-issue psychopath, high on violence in somebody else's country where the deaths of a million people are consigned to cinematic oblivion' (2010). Each of these authors and all the others we will consider throughout this book are equally convinced of the appropriateness of their assertions and each finds evidence within the film to justify and support their argument.

Might one be able to detect this ambiguity of interpretation even in the title chosen for the film? After all, what actually *is* a 'hurt locker'? As one might expect there are a range of definitions of the term and its derivation even became the subject of a hotly contested law suit (see Hinds, 2010). Various understandings of the phrase were offered by members of the cast and crew, reviewers, commentators, academics, and even Bigelow herself, who each seemed to have a different perspective on the matter. Writing in *The Guardian*, Peter Bradshaw, suggested that it 'refers to the physical trauma of being in close proximity, time after time, to the deafening blast of an explosion, controlled or otherwise. That obscene noise and, perhaps just as awful, the tense prelude of compressed silence, encloses you in a tight prison of pain' (2009); Stacey Peebles broadened the definition of the term in her excellent *Welcome to the Suck: Narrating the American Soldier's Experience in Iraq* (2011) arguing that 'the film's title refers to a place of pain, the internal or external experience of suffering that can't be negated by the adrenaline rush of combat. Soldiers often use the phrase to refer to a way of coping with the chaos and confusion of war. After a scalding experience, what can you do that will enable you to get up, go outside the wire, and continue to do your job? Put that experience in the hurt locker, and deal with it later' (2011: 22); Graham Holderness in *Tales from Shakespeare: Creative Collisions* (2014), who detected Shakespearean dimensions to the film's thematic motifs and concurred with Peebles, added that the term should be understood as 'a space of both confinement and agony, a microcosmic "world of pain"' (2014: 119). The actor who played William James, the protagonist of *The Hurt Locker*, Jeremy Renner, had his own understanding of the multiplicities of the term's meaning which he repeated several times in interviews conducted for the film on its release.

> For me, it was a thousand different things and when I first saw it I
> thought that's just a really fucking cool title. Page one, *The Hurt
> Locker*, what is this about?' And then it became a casket, I thought of
> it as a casket or a hospital bed, not as a place. And after shooting it, it
> was an emotional and spiritual place of pain and despair and loneliness
> and loss. This is personal stuff, this is for me, this has nothing to do
> with the movie, that is what it seemed to represent because we were all
> in the hurt locker, somehow. (qtd. in Elfman 2009)

The film, of course, has its own *literal* hurt locker within its diegesis, a
small crate that James keeps under his bed which contains parts from
the numerous bombs he has defused during his many dangerous tours of
duty and even his former wedding ring, of which he remarks 'Like I said...
things which *nearly killed me*'. For the poet Brian Turner, whose poem
'The Hurt Locker' is included in the 2007 collection titled *Here, Bullet* (and
whose work we will return to in Chapter Three), but who is not connected
to the film *The Hurt Locker* in any way, a hurt locker is a metaphor for
the experiences of those who have encountered the horrors of war and he
asks his readers to 'Open the hurt locker and learn how rough men come
hunting for souls' (2007: 11). It is perhaps Kathryn Bigelow's interpretation
of the term which is most significant for us and also the most revealing. In
interviews she repeatedly emphasised the malleability and interpretability
of the phrase and suggested that it was 'a dangerous place, a difficult
place, like if you use it in a sentence, for example, as he [Mark Boal] heard
once, "that if this bomb goes off we'll be in the hurt locker." So it's that
kind of it specifically, but what I liked is its sort of interpretive ability, and
you know that is why it is never really spelt out exactly in the film' (qtd. in
Pendleton, 2013: 191). An interrogation of what this 'interpretive ability'
might mean and why *The Hurt Locker* still resonates for audiences more
than a decade after it was made is the subject of this book.

Chapter 1: The Hollywood War Film and Conflict

> War cinema is as essential to the waging of a war as an M-16 automatic rifle, an aircraft carrier, or a helicopter gunship.
> Guy Westwell, *War Cinema: Hollywood on the Front Line* (2006: 4)

The films that any given national film industry produces about the wars in which it participates should be considered important in a variety of ways. It does not matter whether these films are made in the United States of America, Great Britain, Russia, Germany, Japan or any other country, as affective texts each film crystallises an image of the conflict depicted which remains influential at the time of its release and, perhaps even more importantly, for audiences in the years after it was made. The vast majority of those viewing a war film will not have fought in the conflict they are watching represented on the screen, nor will have they served in the military at all, whether we consider modern wars like those in Iraq and Afghanistan featured in films like *The Hurt Locker* and *American Sniper*, or those from the recent past like the US invasion of Grenada in 1983 featured in *Heartbreak Ridge* (1986), those at the fringes of living memory like *Saving Private Ryan* (1998) and *Fury* (2015), those beyond it by hundreds of years like *The Alamo* (2004) and *Kingdom of Heaven* (2005), or even thousands like *Troy* (2004) and *300* (2006). It is also reasonable to speculate, I would argue, that for a great many people a significant amount of their knowledge and understanding about any particular war comes more from films made about the conflict than text books or even documentaries. Thus, for those of us who never fought in the Second World War it has become embodied in films like *Sands of Iwo Jima* (1949), *Saving Private Ryan* and more recently Christopher Nolan's *Dunkirk* (2017), in artefacts which are embraced and seen by millions more people than will ever read A. J. P. Taylor's *The Origins of the Second World War* (1961), John Keegan's *The Second World War* (1989) or Antony Beevor's *The Second World War* (2012). Given their very contemporary nature, films about the wars in Iraq (2003-2011) and Afghanistan (2001-) are perhaps even more important and have played a vital role in creating an understanding of the conflicts in the cultural imaginary which continues until this day. In this way films about modern wars provide a cultural battleground for interpretations of how they are viewed at the time and how they will be understood by generations to come.

While many regard films to be disposable cultural artefacts, a body of critical scholarship and even empirical evidence exists to persuasively argue the contrary. Alison Landsberg asserts that cinematic texts, rather than being inconsequential, actually function as powerful 'Prosthetic Memories' that are able to give us powerful experiences which both resonate and influence our perception of events just as forcefully as first-hand memories. She states, 'What this suggests is that the experience within the movie theatre and the memories that the cinema affords – despite the fact that the spectator did not live through them – might be as significant in constructing, or deconstructing, the spectator's identity as any experience that s/he has actually lived through' (1995: 180). Andrew Hoskins provides an insight into how this process works in his *Televising War: From Vietnam to Iraq* (2004), describing images or sequences called 'media flash frames' that prove so potent that they can be later misremembered as memories rather than images on a screen. In this understanding of the power of cinema a film like *Saving Private Ryan* operates on multiple levels and should not be understood as 'just a film'. What it does is tell us much more about *how* World War Two was being *remembered* and *understood* in the 1990s when the film was made, towards the end of the Clinton administration (1993-2001), than it actually does about the war itself, for which its relevance is rather superficial. Spielberg's film climaxes with the poignant death of its protagonist Captain John Miller, played by Tom Hanks, an actor who has regularly been described as 'the most trusted man in America' (Collin, 2013), and his dying words to James Francis Ryan (Matt Damon), who his squad has spent almost the entirety of the film looking for (and indeed in some cases dying for) are 'Earn this... Earn it'. These four words were regarded by Albert Auster as having been deliberately formulated to reach beyond the diegetic frames of the screen, reaching out to audiences at the end of the 'American century'. He wrote:

> Although a command directed at Ryan and implicitly his generation that did return from the war, 'earn this' is also a command that resonates far beyond Ryan's generation to the baby boomers and Generations Y and Z. Indeed, every generation of Americans must somehow deserve the sacrifices made at Omaha Beach and other battles in World War Two. Captain Miller's dying words make it possible for future generations to turn the Depression/World War Two generation into the

embodiment of American ideals of self-sacrifice for the twentieth and twenty-first centuries. (2002: 212)

It is quite clear to see that what *Saving Private Ryan* does, first and foremost, is consolidate and reify ideas about the Second World War as a 'mythic summit of national virtue', a clearly defined war of good versus evil, fought for justice and honour rather than the complicated geo-political conflict that it actually was (Hoogland-Noon, 2004: 341). This is how Americans have come to remember it, as a 'Good War' fought by the 'greatest generation' in which the US forces are unambiguously good and the Axis forces of Germany, Japan and Italy are unquestionably evil, in a mythologised conflict in which America wins almost alone and sacrifices a great deal for very little in return, and it is a narrative which has been perpetuated in film after film about the conflict (see Terkel, 1984; Brokaw, 1999). The role of films in the way wars come to be understood then is hard to underestimate, as it is through the cinema that these master narratives are largely constructed in the national imaginary. Thus American films about the Second World War have almost always adopted the same perspective, one in which troubling realities about the conflict, whether that might be concerning American war crimes committed, the racial segregation of the armed forces, the bombings of Dresden and Tokyo (approximately 20,000 and 100,000 civilian deaths respectively), or the use of the atomic bomb on Hiroshima and Nagasaki (almost a quarter of a million killed and wounded) are rarely portrayed onscreen, so far do they depart from the essential tenets of how the war has come to be understood by Americans and are thus elided from the narratives that are created. These ambiguities are not just forgotten, which implies a casual and perhaps even natural process, but more accurately *disremembered*, an active and deliberate procedure in which cultures seek to construct and process the tapestry of their past which has a significant impact on how they see themselves in the present.

Films about the Vietnam War present an even more complicated challenge both for film-makers and audiences, as unlike the Second World War, about which a consensus was quickly reached by Americans, the conflict in Vietnam proved divisive both during and after the years in which it was fought. This might be one of the reasons that, in contrast to films about the Second World War, which were made before, during and after America's participation in the conflict, films about Vietnam were not made (with one or two notable exceptions) until after the war had officially ended in April 1975. What is referred to as the 'Vietnam War cycle' of films began in 1978 with the release of *Coming Home* and *The Deer Hunter*, followed by *Apocalypse Now* in 1979 and into the eighties with films like *First Blood* (1982) before the conflict-defining *Platoon*. What remains clear more than forty years after the cessation of hostilities is that, with little fear of exaggeration, film is the primary medium through which the Vietnam War has come to be understood and remembered by the public. While many have regarded films like *Platoon*, *Full Metal Jacket* (1987) and *Apocalypse Now* to be critical of the Vietnam War, their primary ideological function was actually to 'address and alleviate this trauma in order to restore American self-belief and credibility' (Westwell, 2006: 57). On this affectual power that film possesses to define the parameters of how war comes to be remembered by audiences, Marita Sturken, in her *Tangled Memories: The Vietnam War, the AIDS Epidemic, and the Politics of Remembering* (1997), quoted a Vietnam veteran by the name of William Adams who stated, 'When *Platoon* was first released, a number of people asked me, "Was the war really like that?" I never found an answer... because what "really" happened is now so thoroughly mixed up in my mind with what has been said about what happened that the pure experience is no longer there' (qtd. in Sturken, 1997: 121). It should be asked then that if this is the impact on someone who *actually* served in the war, what might it be on those who only ever experienced it vicariously through the media? As Jeffrey Walsh and Alf Louvre observe in the introduction to *Tell Me Lies About Vietnam* (1988), popular culture representations of these narratives are vital, 'because the suppression of memory, of remembered alternatives, is one means by which dominant views win their power' (1988: 3). Thus, the stories that get told, the perspectives that are offered and the patterns that emerge are incredibly important. In the case of American films about the Vietnam War these patterns were outlined by John Storey in his remarkable 'The articulation of memory and desire: from Vietnam to the war in the Persian Gulf' (2003), which provides a sustained analysis of the tropes of Vietnam War cinema. He argues that films depicting the Vietnam War are characterised by the following: a) Their sustained disconnection from a political or historical understanding of the conflict being fought; b) a committed disavowal of the extent of the US military advantage over the Vietnamese; c) an absence of anti-war sentiment to the extent it was present at the time; d) a predisposition towards forgetting Vietnamese casualties or an almost exclusive focus on American casualties; e) Americanisation of narratives including the pronounced exclusion of Vietnamese who are constructed as an unambiguous Other; f) atrocities committed are portrayed (which gives the appearance of the films being more challenging than they are) but they are presented as isolated acts of madness often brought about by the intense pressure soldiers are placed under; g) the victimisation of the US soldier and by extension the US as a whole (2003: 107). Together these patterns, which can be found in film after film about the conflict from *The Green Berets* (1968) to *We Were Soldiers* (2002) and beyond, construct a narrative about the war which, as Robert Rosenstone suggested, was not just meant to entertain audiences but actually 'designed to reclaim credibility for the military and to rebuild national self-esteem' (2013: 397).

The wars in Iraq and Afghanistan, for a variety of reasons, also had films made about them during and after the conflict, the first of which was arguably *American Soldiers: A Day in Iraq* released as early as August 2005, not much more than two years after the invasion of Iraq in March 2003. Intriguingly, many of the tropes that Storey outlines in his disquisition of films of the Vietnam War are emphatically present in the war films about Iraq and Afghanistan. By 2007-2008 there was a veritable wave of films about these conflicts, including, although not restricted to, *Home of the Brave* (2006), *In the Valley of Elah*, *Grace is Gone* (2007), *Lions for Lambs* (2007), *Redacted* (2007), and *Stop-Loss*, which were followed by the likes of *The Messenger* (2009), *Brothers*, *Green Zone*, *Lone Survivor* (2013) and *American Sniper*. As we have already observed, the majority of these films were largely unsuccessful at the box office and it was not until Clint Eastwood's adaptation of Chris Kyle's autobiographical novel of the same name, *American Sniper* (book 2012, film 2014), that the Iraq war film had a *bona fide* commercial success. *American Sniper* became something of a cultural phenomenon in the US on its release and the subject of both vociferous support and condemnation from those on opposite sides of the political spectrum, but its importance is hard to underestimate. It is, at the time of writing, the most financially successful war film ever made, surpassing even *Saving Private Ryan*. In fact, by way of comparison, its $350 million plus domestic box office total exceeds the returns of *every* film about the Iraq and Afghanistan War *combined* prior to it by a comfortable margin, even if one includes the Academy Award-winning *The Hurt Locker* and Peter Berg's successful *Lone Survivor.*

There is a fairly categorical reason for the financial success of *American Sniper* and that is because it offers a very particular view of the war in Iraq, a vision of how many would like to remember the conflict, about why and how it was fought and who it was fought by, and this is why it was embraced by the American public at large while other films were largely ignored on their release: films like *Redacted* which made just $65,388 at the US box office, *The Messenger* which made $1.1 million, and *Billy Lynn's Long Half-time Walk*, which, despite the presence of a roster of stars like Vin Diesel, Steve Martin, Kristen Stewart, Chris Tucker and being directed by Ang Lee, whose previous film was Academy Award-winning blockbuster success *The Life of Pi* (2012), made only $1.7 million, about four percent of its $40 million budget. *American Sniper* is heavily indebted to American films about World War Two, the Vietnam War and even the Classical Hollywood Western in its portrayal of a just war fought for noble reasons which took a terrible toll not only on those brave American men that participated in it, but also their families who were left behind. It deliberately leaves out explicit references to the broader geo-political realities and context of the conflict in favour of the personal, as has been the case in war films for decades, and as star and co-producer Bradley Cooper suggested, it should be understood as 'just a soldier's story. And on purpose, there's no talk about the war, why we're in it, nothing. It is not what that movie's about' (qtd. in Fleming Jr., 2015). Yet as we will see in our analysis of *The Hurt Locker*, just because a film does not feature explicit references to the politics of the war and the reasons for which it was fought, does not mean at all that it is not deeply rooted in ideology.

American Sniper is one of many films in the rich history of the genre which reproduce a largely uncritical and unreflective narrative of American victimisation, a pronounced disconnection from the complexities of the geo-political arena, and, in some cases, even an elaborate erasure of political and historical context. The primary reason for this is that war films, like the majority of American media products, are not created in a vacuum and many of those that have made a significant impact on audiences have received both privileged access and extensive matériel in exchange for favourable representations of the US military, the cultural implications of which are explored in detail in works like David L. Robb's *Operation Hollywood: How the Pentagon Shapes and Censors the Movies* (2004) and Tricia Jenkins' *The CIA in Hollywood. How the Agency Shapes Film and Television* (2012). Robb and Jenkins explore how such films as *The Right Stuff* (1983), *Pearl Harbor* (2001), *Black Hawk Down* (2001), *Act of Valor* (2012) and *Zero Dark Thirty* (2012) received considerable support which then had a demonstrable impact on how their narratives portrayed the military or governmental agencies like the FBI or the CIA. Perhaps the most pertinent example of this is the Bruckheimer/Simpson production and cold war power fantasy *Top Gun* (1986) which, according to a variety of sources, had a significant impact on Navy recruitment figures after May 1986 due to its overt glamourisation of the subject matter (see Suid, 2002: 500). About the film Douglas Kellner wrote, '*Top Gun* positions the audience in ways to induce spectators to identify or sympathize with its politics; while many of us may resist these positions and may not buy into their ideologies, we must actively resist the text itself' (1995: 80). For many, *Top Gun* might seem to be 'just a movie', but it is quite clear to see how it is a product of the ideological system in which it was made at a very particular time in American history; furthermore, it functions not just as a reflection of these times, but as an active participant in them. So, while modern films might not need the direct approval of a government agency like the OWI (the United States Office of War Information) as they did during the Second World War, a regulatory system exists which decides which films receive support from the military and other government departments and which do not, based on exactly how the films wish to portray them.

From this perspective *The Hurt Locker* has a very interesting production history as it is based on one of three articles written by Mark Boal which were published in *Playboy* (another was turned into the film *In the Valley of Elah* directed by Paul Haggis). 'The Man in the Bomb Suit', published in August/September 2005, was written while Boal was actually an embedded journalist (a reporter offered the opportunity by the government to live and work alongside the military) in an EOD unit in Iraq in 2004. The subsequent screenplay he completed and the film it was intended to become was originally provisionally granted assistance by the Pentagon, but shortly before filming was to commence in Jordan in July 2007 all forms of official support from the military and the United States government were withdrawn. About this decision, Phil Strub, the

Pentagon's special assistant for entertainment media, stated that 'The filmmakers' interest in drama and excitement exceeded what we felt were reasonable realistic portrayals' (qtd. in Barnes, Parker and Horn, 2010). Strub's use of the term 'realistic' here is particularly relevant as it is one that those involved in the production of the film often returned to again and again. Lt. Col. J. Todd Breasseale, who had been scheduled to be the film's military advisor, was reported to have remarked that specifically this was due to scenes in the film 'in which soldiers act violently toward detainees' (ibid.). Boal's subsequent comments about this seem to suggest he regarded this rejection as something of an indication of the film's potency and its credibility which saw *The Hurt Locker* join the ranks of *Full Metal Jacket* and *Apocalypse Now*, films for which Pentagon assistance had also been denied. Boal stated, 'The Department of Defense did not support the movie. And my understanding is that they did not support *Platoon* or *The Deer Hunter*' (ibid.).

Despite the failure of the vast majority of films about the wars in Iraq and Afghanistan to succeed at the box office, they have played a substantial and significant role in how the conflict has been viewed, understood and remembered. Taken together they form a compelling tapestry of how the 'War on Terror' became a central part of American consciousness in the first two decades of the new millennium. It is with this social, political and cultural context provided that we begin our analysis of *The Hurt Locker*.

Chapter 2: The Cinematic Language of *The Hurt Locker*

> The rush of battle is a potent and often lethal addiction, for war is a drug.
> Chris Hedges, *War is a Force that Gives Us Meaning* (2002: 3)

'What can you do with the camera that makes you feel like you're a participant?'

The Hurt Locker begins with the very same epigraph as the one used for this chapter, taken from the Pulitzer Prize-winning journalist Chris Hedges' book *War is a Force that Gives Us Meaning* (2002), in the film presented in white text on a black background. Part of the writing slowly disappears, leaving only the words 'war is a drug' remaining, a concept which emerges as one of the film's central thematic motifs and also a metaphor we will see rendered visually throughout *The Hurt Locker* which also becomes personified in the characterisation and behaviour of its protagonist Sergeant First Class William James. Bigelow and Boal end their quotation from Hedges there, perhaps somewhat conveniently, as in the original book it continues thus:

> ...one I ingested for many years. It is peddled by myth-makers —
> historians, war correspondents, filmmakers, novelists and the state —
> all of whom endow it with qualities it often does possess: excitement,
> exoticism, power, chance to rise above our small stations in life, and
> a bizarre and fantastic universe that has a grotesque and dark beauty.
> It dominates culture, distorts memory, corrupts language and infects
> everything around it. (2002: 3)

Whether Bigelow and Boal join the ranks of these 'myth-makers' that Hedges describes and whether *The Hurt Locker* 'distorts memory' is, in part, the central question of this book. In an episode of Marwan Bishara's *Empire* (Al Jazeera, 2006-) called 'Hollywood and the War Machine' initially broadcast on 9 August 2012, Hedges expressed his profound disappointment with the film, arguing that it had little of substance to say about the Iraq War and that the reason it was given an Academy Award for Best Picture was that it was the first notable film about the war not to be explicitly critical of the conflict.

The Hedges quote is ambiguously presented in *The Hurt Locker* and it should be regarded, of course, as referring primarily to the soldiers featured within its diegesis, but also to us, the audience, who continue to be drawn to stories about war represented onscreen and have been since the likes of *Burial of the Maine Victims* (1898) and *Blanket Tossing a New Recruit* (1898), both directed by William Paley for the Edison Manufacturing Company during its coverage of the Spanish-American War (1898). The idea that war might be a drug is dramatised throughout the narrative of *The Hurt Locker* and also portrayed in its cinematic devices, an aspect that many who have written about the film returned to, such as Amy Taubin who argued that they allowed audiences 'not only to understand the addiction but to feel the adrenaline surge in ourselves' (2009: 35).

The narrative of *The Hurt Locker* formally begins in *media res* with a seven-minute-long sequence which functions effectively as an intense prologue during which we are introduced to not only the EOD team deployed in Iraq, but also the film's visual aesthetic and its thematic motifs. With no credits and only the Hedges quote described above, *The Hurt Locker* abruptly opens with a disorienting FPS (first person shot, that is, as if viewed from the perspective of a particular person or thing) travelling shot filmed in low res and imbued with static, for which no frame of temporal or spatial reference is initially provided for the audience. Lisa Purse suggested the opening shot 'looks like a moonscape in miniature' (2011: 163) and it certainly is otherworldly, with the camera bumping over debris, rocks, rubbish and one conspicuously placed empty can of Pepsi. The only clue initially provided to orient the audience is the diegetic sound of the Arabic call for prayer which plays during the scene and will repeat in moments of tension throughout the film on both its diegetic and non-diegetic soundtrack. This *adhan* (call to worship) which is called by a *mu'addhin* five times a day to summon Muslims for *salat* (ritual prayer) became a very familiar sound to audiences in post-9/11 American film and television shows (see *American Sniper* and *Homeland* [Showtime, 2011-]) and came to function as shorthand for an ominous sense of foreboding quite disconnected from its original religious and cultural context. Corey K. Creekmur argued 'it is employed as a sound of dread, establishing narrative tension through an emphatic aural announcement of the narrative threat unfolding before us' (2010: 87). In Boal's script this moment is described as 'the SOUND of far off GUN SHOTS and CALL to prayer magnify the turmoil of a metropolis in the midst of an occupation/insurgency/civil war' (2013: 2, capitals in original).

Boal's three part definition of the conflict in Iraq is an interesting one, suggestive of a multiplicity of perspectives that *The Hurt Locker* actually avoids, portraying the conflict and those who participate in it in a very particular way from its opening image until its last.

Figure 1

After a few seconds it is revealed that the shots are actually footage from an ANDROS bomb disposal robot and we are located somewhere in Baghdad, Iraq, in 2004. American soldiers and members of the ICDF (Iraqi Civil Defense Force) are shown hurrying crowds away from the vicinity of what is suspected to be an IED (Improvised Explosive Device) in the middle of a busy street. The cinematography in the sequence, as it will be throughout the film, is characterised by its largely hand-held nature, under the guidance of director of photography Barry Ackroyd, who Bigelow collaborated with again almost ten years later on *Detroit* (2017). Ackroyd honed his Realist aesthetic early in his career with the Ken Loach films *Riff-Raff* (1991) and *Raining Stones* (1993) before working in the American film industry with Paul Greengrass on *United 93* (2006) prior to *The Hurt Locker* and *Green Zone*, *Captain Philips* (2013) and *Jason Bourne* (2016) after.

This very particular cinematic style is evident from the first shots and could accurately be described as both jagged and frenetic. This embrace of the immediacy of the hand-held technique was very frequently used in the first decade of the new millennium and beyond in a variety of genres that I have elsewhere described as 'the quintessential new millennial marker of authenticity' (McSweeney, 2014: 48). Within these parameters Ackroyd utilises a range of devices: partially obscured imagery, imprecise and off-kilter framing, whip pans, transgressions of the 180-degree rule, snap zooms and snap reverse zooms (sometimes multiple and the same shot). All of these result in a cinematic aesthetic which remains profoundly unstable even in close ups and insert shots which are traditionally steadier even in more action-oriented genres, and have a corresponding effect for audiences. It is a camera which rarely pauses and whose tempo and fluidity is only matched by the pace of the editing by Chris Innis and Bob Murawski, who also won an Academy Award for their contribution to the film. The first two minutes alone are comprised of more than forty-four separate shots, the cumulative effect of which is a profound sense of disorientation on the part of the viewer as the film's fictional spaces are shown to be threatening even before the central narrative of the film has begun. Lisa Purse wrote that the result of this was that 'the camera and the editing also [communicate] the volatility of the situation, which we will learn is based on the difficulty of 'making sense' of who is a threat and who is an innocent bystander. In this way aesthetic choices work through the body to allow the audience to experience first-hand this environment's alienating inscrutability as well as its contingency' (2011: 164).

The efficacy of this stylistic approach is enhanced by the fact that *The Hurt Locker* was not filmed on a studio backlot in the United States but in Jordan, a country which borders Iraq to the west and has a very similar architecture to Baghdad where the film is primarily set. Shooting in Jordan also gave the production access to a great many Iraqi refugees who had fled the war, enabling many of the film's supporting characters and extras to be played by Iraqi civilians with first-hand experience of the conflict. The production itself, as described by many of those involved, was as intense as the cinematography of the opening scenes. It was filmed over a brisk forty-four day schedule with four 16mm cameras running simultaneously over an extremely large set in which actors were often not informed how the scenes would be shot, resulting in more than two hundred hours of footage that needed to be edited down to the film's final one hundred and thirty-one minute running time. Steven Jay Rubin, in his *Combat Films: American Realism, 1945-2010* (2011), reported that Bigelow 'wouldn't necessarily tell the actors where they [the cameras] were' (2011: 273), something confirmed by Jeremy Renner in an interview who said, 'We had cameras everywhere...We called them Ninja cameras, just hiding all over the place' (qtd. in Boal, 2013: 119). These aesthetic choices produce an undeniably intense result and one which Kathryn Bigelow described as 'an experiential form of film-making' (qtd. in Hond, 2013: 205) that is self-consciously designed to recreate, as far as possible for audiences, what it *felt like to be there*, in a similar way to the D-Day beach landing was constructed in Spielberg's *Saving Private Ryan*, the withdrawal from Dunkirk in Nolan's Dunkirk, or the Battle of Okinawa in Mel Gibson's *Hacksaw Ridge* (2016). In an interview about his approach to the film Barry Ackroyd used a range of terms that were to be often repeated by Kathryn Bigelow and Mark Boal concerning the film's construction:

> The first thing was to go to a place as *realistic* as possible. We couldn't go to Iraq, so we chose Jordan: the buildings and the minarets looked the same; the extras had the same basic bone structure – Middle Eastern, not North African. Kathryn [Bigelow, director] wanted the kind of *verisimilitude* I had provided on *United 93*. Long takes with more than one camera observing the characters. We don't break it down into storyboards; you don't second-guess where the honest angle would be, you let things happen. That *naturalism* comes from my background with Ken Loach. If you're out of focus on a moment such as an explosion, it just makes it more *real*. (qtd. in Hoad, 2017, my italics)

The impact of this approach in *The Hurt Locker* was frequently returned to by commentators: Amy Taubin suggested that it put audiences 'in the middle of a fully three-dimensional theater of war with mines underfoot and snipers everywhere' (Taubin 2009: 34) and Robert Burgoyne claimed that it immersed 'the spectator in the heightened sensory experience of a space that contains threats from every direction – from above ground and below, from near and far' (2012: 14).

Figure 2

The opening scene also introduces to us to the film's characters, some of whom will become its protagonists: the genial Staff Sergeant Matthew

Thompson (Guy Pearce) who is shown to be friendly and open, eating a chocolate bar while interacting in an amiable way with his subordinates in the team who include the proficient and level headed Sergeant J.T. Sanborn (Anthony Mackie) and the young but capable Specialist Owen Eldridge (Brian Geraghty).[1] Sanborn is the first of the three we see, but he is not introduced with anything resembling a traditional establishing shot of the group, but instead in a tight close up of his face looking to the right of the screen, followed by a similarly constricted close up (with a snap zoom as part of the shot) of Thompson a few shots later. The first shot which has both of them in the same image is also an odd one as it has a large portion of the frame, roughly fifty percent, obscured by a figure out of focus in the foreground to the right, which a few seconds later is shown to be Eldridge. The team identify, with the help of the ANDROS robot, a suspected IED and engage in some humorous banter which involves them joking about the size of their 'dicks' until they realise how serious the bomb is which could, as Thompson suggests 'do some fucking damage'. Thompson decides the safest way to dispose of it is to use the ANDROS robot to remotely park detonators in its proximity and then explode the device with both the EOD team and any civilians far away from danger. However, on its way towards the bomb one of the wheels of the wagon designed to complete the task falls off, leading to one of the rare occasions, as diluted as it is, that *The Hurt Locker* offers a criticism of the wider parameters of the war. Thompson asks Eldridge, 'Did *you* build that?' to which he replies, 'No, the US army did!' and later he will sarcastically ask Sanborn,

> Aren't you glad the Army has all these tanks parked here? Just in case the Russians come and we have to have a big tank battle?... I mean, anyone comes alongside a Humvee, we're dead. Anybody even looks at you funny, we're dead. Pretty much the bottom line is, if you're in Iraq, you're dead. How's a fucking tank supposed to stop that?

Somewhat surprisingly, given the divisive nature of the war in Iraq, these two fairly muted comments are the extent to which the army and the war itself are directly discussed. It is this lack of explicit commentary that led to many writers calling the film 'apolitical' (see Denby, 2009; Smith, 2009; Barker, 2011). Those looking for more criticism of the war or the reasons for which it was fought have to look for it elsewhere in the film: in subtext, metaphor, association and allusion.

Figure 3

It is only the failure of the ANDROS robot which prompts Thompson to reluctantly put on the cumbersome bomb disposal suit and approach the bomb on foot. Sanborn asks him, 'You don't like waiting around here in this beautiful neighbourhood? to which he replies sarcastically, 'I *love* it.' It is very clear Thompson and the team prefer the safety of the robot and the suit is used only as a last resort after *every other avenue* has been pursued. Even while using the suit Thompson tells the team that he will set a trigger near the device rather than try to disarm the bomb so that they can BIP it (a military term meaning 'Blow in Place') from a safe distance. As Thompson slowly moves towards the IED the team establish constant communication with each other in what seems to be a well-established routine and standard procedure during which Thompson repeatedly relays to them updates on his position, his proximity to the explosive device, observations about his surroundings and even how he is feeling, using his call sign Blaster One, with both Sanborn and Eldridge doing the same.

The sequence described above continues to be filmed hand-held by cinematographer Barry Ackroyd in the same style which we have seen characterised in the film's opening moments. It is not only the film's visual design which contributes to this sense of immersion, as the soundscape of *The Hurt Locker* is similarly intense and also participates in this experiential approach to cinema, starting with the call to prayer already mentioned, but heightened by the diegetic sounds of the crowds, gun shots in the distance, helicopters and planes passing overhead and even the amplified noise of Thompson's breathing and his heart-beat which are layered over shots taken directly from his point of view, some of which are shown through the visor of the protective bomb suit. These sounds were both created and coordinated by sound designer Paul N.J. Ottosson who won not one Academy Award, but two for his contribution to the film, one for Best Achievement in Sound Mixing and another for Best Achievement in Sound Editing (with Ray Beckett). Ottosson stated,

> No matter where you are in the movie we try to put you in a situation, wherever you are, there's sound all the way around you. I was in the military for a year and a half and a lot of times you don't see the enemy, when you hear something you need to identify what this is very quickly and if this is a friend or not. That's the sound; we try to create this 360° world of uncertainty because that's how it is. You look at some of these shots, you see a guy in a building, is it someone looking at me or going to take a shot at me? That was really important for the movie to always remind you where you are, that you're in the movie, that you're not watching a movie... I'm putting you directly in the drama, its events, and where it's located. (qtd. in Koppl)

As Ottosson observes, these creative devices are utilised to both enhance the immersion felt by the audience and, somewhat paradoxically, the film's authenticity of experience. Bigelow suggested, 'You want to make it as *real* and as *authentic* as possible, to put the audience into the Humvee, into a boots-on-the-ground experience. How do you do that? You do it by finding a look, a feel, and a texture that is very immediate, raw, and vital, and yet is also not anesthetized. I wanted, as a filmmaker, to sort of step aside and let just the rawness and integrity of the subject be as pronounced as possible and not have it feel sort of "cinematic"' (qtd. in Dawson, 145, my italics). The majority of these devices employed that we have already noted are those firmly associated with the Realist mode of film-making: from the jagged, documentary-style of its cinematography to the film's general lack of recognisable stars (Jeremy Renner and Anthony Mackie were relatively unknown at the time), and its episodic, fragmentary and non-traditional narrative structure which we will see as our analysis of the film continues. This was something returned to in commentaries written about *The Hurt Locker*, many of which seemed as if they were contractually obliged to use the term 'realistic' in their descriptions of the film with many going so far as to compare it to a documentary. A.O. Scott stated that it emphasised a 'hyperbolic realism, [which] distils the psychological essence and moral complications of modern warfare into a series of brilliant, agonizing set pieces' (2010); Rainer described a 'documentarylike immediacy' (2009); Trafton said that it brought a 'documentary approach to the war experience' (2016: 61) which was both 'soulful and realistic' and also according to Jeansonne and Luhrssen 'achieved something more real than anything a documentary crew could have captured' (2014: 159).[2] These descriptions of *The Hurt Locker* seem to confirm Bigelow's desire to produce a film which was 'really meant to be reportorial. And to put you where the journalist was. And however you're feeling ideologically, politically, about it, I think it gives you the opportunity to appreciate these men in this job' (qtd. in Horton, 2013: 151-152).

Yet this categorical embrace of the film's realism is decidedly problematic for a variety of reasons as Realism as an aesthetic should be understood, first and foremost, as a cinematic style rather than *an absence of one* in a way that does not seem to be acknowledged by any of the writers above. While this approach, on the surface, seems to offer no political commentary, to confuse Realism with apoliticism is certainly naïve. As John Fiske reminds us, Realism is just as much an aesthetic conceit as other modes of artistic expression. He suggests,

> The conventions of realism have developed in order to disguise the constructedness of the 'reality' it offers, and therefore of the arbitrariness of the ideology that is mapped onto it. Realism is beguiling for audiences who are like to confuse such mimetic stylistic techniques with some sort of ideological neutrality. Grounding ideology in reality is a way of making it appear unchallengeable and unchangeable, and thus is a reactionary political strategy. (2011: 36)

The range of techniques employed by Ackroyd then, whether it might be the extensive use of the handheld camera, the deliberately obscured or blurred imagery, the process of frequently shooting *through* objects and the immediacy these cinematic devices results in, gives the *appearance* of being realistic, but does not result in a film more *inherently real* than any other.

It should be observed that the experiential and Realist aesthetic constructed by *The Hurt Locker* is a very particular and subjective experience, one that is restricted exclusively to portraying and prioritising the perspectives of the US soldiers that the film focuses on and who emerge as its central characters. This is perhaps to be expected given that it is an American film, financed and produced by American production companies, and also written and directed by Americans. However, when almost every single war film set in Iraq and Afghanistan adopts these very same perspectives, closer inspection of the impact of these decisions is required. Bigelow's utilisation of the aesthetic we have described combined with numerous close ups of the anxious faces of the EOD squad, each of whom are given a name, a personality and a certain amount of psychological depth and background to their characterisation, and the intermittent use of POV shots, whether through the visor of the bomb disposal suit helmet or through the cross hairs of Eldridge's or Sanborn's automatic rifles, results in a film which sutures the audience with *their* experiences. Even the film's diegetic and non-diegetic soundtrack is designed to promote a 'claustrophobic identificatory relation with the soldiers' (Bennet and Diken, 2011: 170) and to ensure that each person in the audience, according to Ottosson, was to feel like they were 'the fourth man on the team' (qtd. in Grove, 2010) or as Barry Ackroyd put it, 'We were always asking ourselves, "What can you do with the camera that can make you feel like you're a participant?"' (qtd. in '*The Hurt Locker* Production Notes') The cumulative effect of these stylistic and narrative choices is to bind spectators to the experiences and perspectives of the soldiers at the same time as refusing to portray Iraqi characters in anything other than superficial ways, as Iraqis are pushed to the margins of the screen or erased entirely from the film's narrative. Furthermore, the location of the narrative in a bomb disposal team itself is not a neutral one, even though it appears to be on the surface, but rather allows the film to disconnect itself from the day-to-day realities of combat and portray a war in which the US are not combatants but peacekeepers, committed to saving Iraqi lives rather than taking them, the popular impression that many Americans had about the war in its early years. By concentrating on the intense pressure that the US soldiers are under, the film narrows 'the war to the existential confrontation of man and deadly threat' and the audience is free to enjoy the destruction 'without ambivalence and guilt' (Denby, 2009: 84). These creative choices have a number of ramifications which we will explore in more detail in Chapter Two, chief of which might be both the prioritisation of American viewpoints on the conflict and the negation of the experiences of the Iraqi Other, decisions which, it is very clear to see, are *far from apolitical* in nature. In actual fact, on closer consideration, *The Hurt Locker* can be seen to present a distinctly conservative ideological approach to the conflict, as the American mission in Iraq is framed as a humanitarian, even altruistic one, with its protagonists, all members of the EOD, tasked with preventing insurgents from killing Iraqi civilians, destroying Iraqi buildings and homes at great risk to their own personal safety. The target of the bombs is rarely shown as being the Americans themselves, which, of course, was the frequent reality on the ground (see Greenstock, 2017). This transformation of a contentious political narrative into a more personal one initially seems to be a retreat from ideology, but in reality is also far from it. Whether it is true, as Slavoj Žižek suggested, that *The Hurt Locker* contains 'ideology at its purest' asserting that 'the focus on the perpetrator's traumatic experience enables us to obliterate the entire ethico-political background of the conflict' (2010), is not entirely clear, but what *is* clear is that the film is very much a political text grounded and immersed in ideology despite the assurances of the contrary from the people who made it. Thus, comments like Martin Barker's that 'The film stripped out almost every single moment that might be judged political. I cannot recall seeing one US flag in the entire film – usually the first marker of such politics. There are no moments of inserted speech, or television coverage, or soldiers' debates about why they are there' (2011: 156) and others like it show a striking misunderstanding of how contemporary American films about war operate. Contemporary war films, in general, do not embrace ideology in such explicit fashions as they might have done some decades ago, but their political perspectives are subsumed into their narratives and the characters which they portray and, as we have seen, the cinematic devices they use to tell their stories.

Despite Rubin's suggestion that 'one of the first things you notice about the bomb-disposal sequences in *The Hurt Locker* is that there is no artifice in filming them' (2011: 268), such unreserved acceptance of the film's claims fails to recognise that the techniques employed, many of which we have outlined in this first chapter, are quite far from having 'no artifice', something which becomes more apparent as the film's prologue reaches its climax. As Thompson reaches the bomb the pace of the editing begins to quicken. Sanborn, who is on 'top cover' duty, that is the primary point of observation and support for Thompson's precarious position, is approached by an Iraqi man who starts to ask him questions about where he is from, but Sanborn curtly sends him away with a 'Get out of here, man, this ain't a fucking meet and greet!' The man's expression as he leaves the area is certainly coded as suspicious and the implication the audience is left with is that he might have had something to do with the traumatic event which is about to take place.

When Thompson reaches twenty-five meters from the IED, which Sanborn identifies as 'the kill zone', he retrieves the detonators and places them next to the bomb. It is then that Eldridge identifies another suspicious looking man, who is described as 'the Butcher' in the screenplay and the film's credits, holding a phone to his face, which Eldridge believes might be able to detonate the bomb. This Butcher had been introduced very briefly earlier in the scene with two throwaway shots unlikely to have been noticed by the audience as he was angrily ushered away from his shop by soldiers. He is even given a suggestive and crudely simplistic close up of his face where his eyes look suitably malevolent. The Butcher is the first in a long line of unsympathetic Iraqi characterisations of which the film will offer little variation: they are mostly categorically evil or victims that require saving by virtuous Americans, with not much room for anywhere else on the spectrum between these two poles. Eldridge runs towards the Butcher pointing his rifle at him while yelling, 'Put down the phone!' at the same time as Sanborn tells him to 'Burn him!' as the editing progresses to a frenetic pace. The EOD team is shown as right to be suspicious, *as they always are* in the film, as an insert of the Butcher's hand shows him pressing a button on the phone and detonating the bomb.

The presentation of the resulting explosion in which Thompson is caught and subsequently dies at around the seven-minute mark seems to go against what we have established as the Realist aesthetic of the film thus far, in a series of shots, eight of which are in extreme slow motion. There is a shot of the ground undulating as the pressure wave of the detonation courses through the earth, one of rust being dislodged from the roof of an abandoned (and perhaps previously exploded) car, and several of the explosion itself. The detonation, rather than being played out in linear time, is shown repeating quickly four separate times in what might be interpreted as a nod to affective Eisensteinian montage techniques (see Thomson, 2005:120-135). The final shot of the sequence shows Thompson lying still on the floor also in slow motion, the audience having seen the character who many might have presumed to be the film's central protagonist, killed. As striking and beautifully framed as they are they do

Figure 4

Figure 5

offer something of a challenge to Bigelow's claims that 'these men [in *The Hurt Locker*] arguably have the most dangerous job in the world, so what they're doing is inherently, incredibly dramatic and intense. So I don't need to make what they're doing more dramatic' (qtd. in Horton, 2013: 151) or Rubin's that Bigelow did not 'impose an aesthetic' on its subject matter (2011: 268). The prologue is a tremendously visceral and vividly constructed sequence but to regard it as reportorial, apolitical and without artifice is problematic to say the least.

Thompson's unexpected death, especially considering he is played by the most high-profile member of the cast (perhaps alongside Ralph Fiennes, who is also later unexpectedly and rather unceremoniously killed) is an indication to the audience that the world of *The Hurt Locker* is an incredibly dangerous one and that extra-diegetic celebrity status is no guarantee of survival. Like the unanticipated deaths of characters like Marion Crane (Janet Leigh) in *Psycho* (1960), Vincent Vega (John Travolta) in *Pulp Fiction* (1994), Jack Vincennes (Kevin Spacey) in *L.A Confidential* (1997) and Julian (Julianne Moore) in *Children of Men* (2004), audiences are challenged by a potent narrative device which, in the case of *Psycho*,

Hemmeter argued, 'strips the narrative of the structured coherence and continuity' (2011: 72). Bigelow described Thompson's death and this prologue sequence as a whole which we have described as 'a learning curve for the audience' (qtd. in Rubin, 2011: 271) and it is one that looms over the rest of the film, that in this world *anyone* can die at *any moment*, and they certainly do: later the unnamed British mercenary played by Ralph Fiennes is killed rather unheroically in the middle of a firefight in the desert, as is the good natured but ineffectual Dr Cambridge (Christian Camargo), who leaves the safety of Camp Victory to see what the 'real' war is like at the behest of Eldridge, and is exploded by an IED which leaves literally nothing left of him behind.

Figure 6

Figure 7

Sergeant William James the 'wild man!', and Iraq as the New Wild West Frontier

After the death of Thompson, Sanborn and Eldridge are assigned a new squad leader, Sergeant First Class William James, who ultimately emerges as the film's primary protagonist. It is his experiences we will follow most closely and it was his face used most often on the posters and marketing for the film, with even the film's title primarily a reference to him more than anyone else. It is immediately apparent that James is extremely different to Thompson, in terms of his manner, his attitude and his approach to military procedure, both on the battlefield and off, and it is the friction that this creates between him and the rest of the squad that provides the drama on which much of the film is centred.

In cinematic terms James is introduced slightly more conventionally than the team had been in the prologue, as he is first seen in his quarters listening to loud heavy metal music by the band Ministry, with their song 'Khyber Pass' (from the album *Rio Grande Blood*, 2006) playing on the film's diegetic soundtrack, a type of music which became heavily associated with the American military in the conflicts in Iraq and Afghanistan. J. Martin Daughtry, the author of *Listening to War: Sound, Music, Trauma and Survival in Wartime Iraq* (2015), even reported that in Iraq American soldiers would 'jack their iPods into the LRAD [long range acoustic devices], and blast AC/DC and other loud music at groups of Iraqis whom they wanted to disperse' (2015: 242).[3] It is a style of music with which James will be repeatedly connected to throughout the film and a genre, as Waksman suggests, that is 'widely recognized for its masculine connotations' (2011: 196). Sanborn advises James not to remove the protective wooden boards from the windows of his quarters, reminding him that the base is frequently attacked by enemy mortars and that fragments could easily smash through the glass if it is left unprotected, but James merely shrugs and only offers, "I like the sunshine", in reply.

It is with this line and the following scenes that the audience realises that the film's epigraph by Chris Hedges is primarily about James and it is for him above all that 'war is a drug'. After a brief exchange James cuts Sanborn off, with the script suggesting that he 'has reached his intimacy limit' (2013: 16) and it is clear James is uncomfortable communicating with people, something accentuated in Boal's screenplay in its introduction of the character, which notes

> Though a former US Army Ranger in his early thirties, fit and good-looking, one of the lucky ones, he possesses an unusual demeanor. In a world of outgoing young men, James seems markedly self-absorbed.

Sanborn notices this trait instantly and is puzzled by it. The truth is that after so many years down range, racking up kills and disarming bombs, James has lost some of the ability and most of the need to connect to other people. (2013: 15)

This is shown more clearly in their first active EOD operation together as a unit shortly after. The squad, now comprised of James, Sanborn and Eldridge, drive through the city of Baghdad which is shown as a threatening space even when the team are not in the tense environment of a bomb disposal situation. An onscreen caption reveals that there are now thirty-eight days left in their rotation, and perhaps somewhat ironically it is the only countdown that a film about bomb disposal will feature on its screens. Eldridge mans the heavy machine gun on top of the Humvee calling out to vehicles to get out of their way in simplistic Arabic phrases that became familiar to American audiences throughout the decade, 'Yalla' and 'Imshi', two words that find their way into many films about Iraq and can be broadly translated as 'hurry up' and 'go away'. He throws an empty water bottle at the car in front of him to make it go faster even though it is clear that it and all the other cars are stuck in traffic. There are more unsettling shots through objects which give a sense of them being watched and under threat *all of the time*; one of a lame cat running across the road, another of a man hurriedly carrying around a corner what appears to be a stolen television set and many of ordinary Iraqi civilians on the street who almost all look vaguely threatening, even the women and children, only going about their daily business. The team are called to a situation where a unit of American soldiers have reported a bomb threat, but when they get there all they are able to see is a refuse-filled street and an empty Humvee as the film portrays what will become a habitual process of showing the bustling and crowded Baghdad streets quickly emptied, transforming it into a ghost town when it is required by the film's narrative, a process which becomes more noticeable as the film progresses and also disputes the film's claims towards 'Realism'. It is James who notices tiny American flags waving from an Iraqi backyard and he is the one who will notice almost everything of importance throughout the film.

It is here we see begin to see the real differences between the operational procedure of Thompson and James: whereas Thompson was clearly shown to prefer the safety of the ANDROS robot and only put on the uncomfortable bomb suit as a last resort *after the robot was disabled*, James immediately reaches for it with a nonchalant, 'I'll take care of it'. An incredulous Sanborn protests, 'You know you don't have to go down there, man, we already have the bot half way out,' but James, as he does many times in the film, merely ignores his squad mate and walks off down the street clad in the bulky suit laughing, with only a 'Let's rock and roll man!' tossed off to his team behind him. In the prologue we had seen Thompson's careful approach to a suspected IED marked with a clear set of precise measurements and commands ('Okay. I'm going to make my approach. This area looks okay. No power-lines. Clean line of sight'), but James does not offer these comments or anything like them to his team; in fact, he refuses to communicate on the radio, nor does he call out markers and he even unexpectedly throws a smoke grenade without telling them to obscure his position from any enemies who might be observing him. He shrugs off the need to communicate with his team with, 'Are we going on a *date*, Sanborn?' When Sanborn asks to be informed of the suspected location of the IED, James answers, 'Hell, I don't know. I'll let you know when I'm standing over it.' Both Sanborn and Eldridge have recognised by the film's seventeenth minute that James' method is far from standard operating procedure: Eldridge comments 'He's a rowdy boy' and Sanborn concurs with 'He's *reckless*.' Later back at the base James will tell Sanborn, 'You'll get it though, *you'll get it...*', an ambiguous line which at the time we the audience are perhaps expected to understand as evidence of his arrogance and presumption but which is complicated later as the film progresses.

While Thompson had sarcastically suggested 'I *love* it...', it is clear that James is actually drawn to bomb disposal for reasons the film asks the audience to speculate about, but will never actually provide an answer. When challenged about his unconventional behaviour he only offers, 'Hey, this is combat!' Only Sanborn and Eldridge will be shown to criticise his actions throughout the film and, as we will see, as the latest in a long line of rule breaking maverick American heroes, James definitely gets results. As he is approaching the suspected bomb the film offers him another way to display his composure in dangerous situations as an Iraqi taxi is shown speeding through a US army roadblock and coming to a stop just a few feet in front of him. The film keeps the driver out of the centre of the frame and at first in almost complete darkness even though it is completely light outside as the scene takes place in the middle of the day. The taxi driver is introduced with an extreme close up of his eyes via a cracked rear-view mirror in a similar way used to emphasise the Butcher's perfidy in the film's prologue. *The Hurt Locker* has little interest in who this man is, what his motivations might be, or even his name (he is not even included in the credits). Why the man would choose to behave in such a way appears to be irrelevant to Bigelow and Boal – he is just another one of the film's threatening Iraqis, whether they are men, women or children, who do not exist to do anything other than provide a threat to the soldiers and allow James to demonstrate his steely poise under moments of intense pressure and his proficiency as a soldier. James' calm is contrasted with the panic of not only Sanborn and Eldridge, who yell over the radio, but also the soldiers at the checkpoint, who are similarly shown as unsure what to do. It is only James who remains entirely in control throughout the scene; as he slowly draws his pistol his only words to them over the radio are '*I got it*'. In an image reminiscent of that which has been historically called a 'Mexican standoff' (see Selbo, 2015: 247), the likes of which have featured in the Western genre for decades, James is shown facing the taxi and inside it a driver who refuses to speak, communicate or move the vehicle. James first shoots at the ground around the car ordering him to get back, then shoots the windscreen, but the driver is only shown to acquiesce when James presses his pistol to the man's forehead. Boal and Bigelow even provide James with what might be regarded as something of a 'one liner' after the driver departs, one that would not have been out of place in an action film from the 1980s – 'Well, if he wasn't an insurgent he sure the hell is now' – which, while it seems somewhat out of place, suggests a degree of self-awareness about his behaviour that will be returned to from time to time throughout the course of the film.

The IED that James then finds after the taxi departs is not just a single explosive device, but a series of linked bombs connected together in what is referred to by the EOD as a 'daisy chain'. The crane shot which looms over James as he pulls them all out of the rubble at the same time, revealing them as encircling him, was an image used often in the film's marketing and publicity, and even in variations of its poster. He is watched by yet another suspicious Iraqi from the building overlooking his position on the street in a range of shots which heavily imply this man is the one who constructed and planted the bomb (the character is referred to only

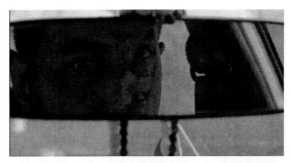

Figure 8

Figure 9

in the credits as 'Insurgent in Stairwell' and played by Wasfi Amour).
When the insurgent sees James start to defuse the bomb, with the
Arabic call to prayer introduced into the soundtrack again at this point
in an example of when it is not entirely clear whether it is diegetic or
non-diegetic, he is shown to drop the detonator and run away, passing a
small child in the stairwell who might have been killed by the explosion
the man was planning, as the film offers us very clearly defined examples
of what *cowards do* and what *heroes do*. James and the insurgent even
have a brief moment of eye contact with one another as James holds
up the 'primer' to show him that he has outsmarted his opponent,
as he will always be shown to win throughout the film. The film has
established quite clearly a spectrum of behaviour for its characters in
the first twenty minutes of its narrative with heroic Americans on one
side, willing to risk their own lives to save those of Iraqi women and
children, and unquestionably, unconscionably evil Iraqi insurgents/
terrorists on the other, those who choose to place bombs on the streets
of Baghdad for no other reason than to kill innocents. This juxtaposition
is a powerful embodiment of what the film would have us understand

is the stark difference between the noble and altruistic bravery of the average American soldier and the cruelty of the Iraqi insurgent. It is a simplistic dichotomy the film will return to several times and one of many illustrations which underlines one of the central assertions of this book, that while *The Hurt Locker* may not feature triumphant waving American flags or speeches about the war, it is far from an apolitical text.

Figure 10

The next bomb the team are called to the day after is immediately coded by the film as not 'just' another explosive device by the side of the road, but something much more serious. It is hidden inside a suspicious looking vehicle parked in the vicinity of the United Nations building in Baghdad which is identified in the script as the 'UNITED NATIONS TEMPORARY HEADQUARTERS' (2013: 32). While the events featured in the sequence which follows are fictional they cannot help but evoke the real-life suicide truck bombing which targeted the United Nations Assistance Mission at the Canal Hotel in Iraq on August 19 2003 which killed twenty-two and wounded over one hundred, one of which was UN Special Representative Sergio Vieira de Mello. It was this event which directly resulted in the withdrawal of six hundred United Nations staff from Iraq. In the film's version of the events, as the team approach the vehicle they come under fire from an insurgent on an overlooking rooftop who shoots at the car in what one presumes is an attempt to detonate the bomb. The camera reveals dozens of innocent Iraqi civilians being rushed from the building as US soldiers arrive to help. James quickly demotes Sanborn from the position of 'top cover' in favour of the more junior Eldridge, in what seems to be a direct response to Sanborn challenging his unconventional procedure on the previous mission and calling James a 'redneck piece of trailer trash'.

As in the two previous sequences featuring the bomb disposal team, Bigelow frames the IED in a very public space, leaving the team exposed from all directions, with many suspicious looking Arabs observing their movements and actions. One man is even shown to be recording them with a hand-held camera as Eldridge remarks 'getting ready to put me on YouTube' and later the man appears to be communicating with others on the tower of a minaret which leads Sanborn to suspect the whole thing might be part of a trap. As Bruce Bennett and Bülent Diken wrote, 'The experience of moving through Iraq is, for the soldiers, an experience of being perilously visible, objectified and on display' (2011: 170). This process, in some ways, is key to how audiences are asked to understand the precarity of the EOD's role in Baghdad and one might speculate, the role of the United States in Iraq as a whole. The film does not show the US as an occupying force, not one that should be considered as the world's most powerful military despite the fact that in 2005, the year the film is set, according to US government figures, the country spent more than $491 billion on its armed forces, a figure that, by the time of the film's release in 2009 had risen to $698 billion (see Chantrill, n.d.s). As has often been repeated, this figure is the equivalent to the next seven largest military budgets combined. *The Hurt Locker* presents an image of the US military very different to this, as do the majority of the films about the wars in Iraq and Afghanistan. Rather, American soldiers are shown to be an under-resourced, plucky group of men in constant danger from a powerful and impossible to identify enemy force. Of course, this is quite a substantial reversal of power relations from the real world to screen, but it is one which has been promulgated by American films about its wars since the birth of the medium. In this screen war, which we might regard as something of an alternate reality or allohistorical narrative, American soldiers are not the perpetrators of violence but its victims, and it is the American soldier who is the true casualty of a war which is fought for honourable reasons against a morally corrupt enemy seeking to prevent Americans from saving the lives of women and children. This is not to say that American soldiers did not find themselves in such situations, but the frequency of their portrayals and the refusal to offer Iraqis any comparable sense of humanity emerges as problematic. This understanding of the conflict to which media depictions of the war make a powerful contribution, portrays Americans under constant threat and danger, which is the way the war came to be understood by the American public at large, with a conscious and one might say wilful lack of acknowledgement of the hundreds of thousands of Iraqis wounded, killed and displaced by the conflict. The film, as do almost all films about the conflict made in the west, at best pushes Iraqi experiences of the war to the side-lines and at worst erases them entirely.

Sanborn recognises the precarity of their situation outside the United Nations building and suggests 'We got a lot of eyes on us, James. We need to get out of here.' But James refuses, as he seems to view every bomb as both a personal challenge and an opportunity to test himself on the battlefield. He deviates from established protocol even further than he did in the previous mission as not only does he refuse to use the ANDROS robot, but he also takes off the headphones the team uses to communicate with one another after becoming annoyed by Sanborn's repeated requests for updates. Perhaps most surprisingly he also even removes the protective bomb suit itself with a justification that seems to be a very 'movie-like' line of dialogue, even more so than the previous mission's 'Well, if he wasn't an insurgent he sure the hell is now'. He tells Eldridge, 'There's enough bang in here to send us all to Jesus. If I'm gonna die, *I want to die comfortable.*' The audience knows that this is a *serious* bomb, not just because of its proximity to the UN building but because James says 'Oh God' when he first sees it and drops his wrench to the floor. Again, he remains calm and collected, while Eldridge and Sanborn become progressively more concerned about their dangerous situation. Even when Sanborn informs him that the area has been evacuated of all civilians and that protocol suggests they should leave, allowing the engineers to detonate the bomb without danger, James refuses. After several minutes of looking inside the car, cutting away piece after piece of it, he finally locates the device and successfully deactivates it, slumping back in the Humvee for what is coded as a post-coital-like cigarette with the line 'That was *good...*' It is then Sanborn abruptly punches him in the face, telling him 'Never turn your head set off again!' an action which has been described as unrealistic by several servicemen and EOD members (see Hoit, 2010; Smith, 2010).

It is not only crowds of threatening Arabs that have been watching James disarm the bomb but also a US army Colonel by the name of Reed (David Morse), who approaches the EOD team, impressed by James' actions and his bravery. Reed expresses his admiration – 'That's just hot shit!

Figure 11

You're a *wild man* you know that?' – and asks James how many bombs he has defused. The answer, which James only very reluctantly provides, is revealed to be eight hundred and seventy-three. Reed's manner and his behaviour connect him to the similarly framed man of action, James, and prior to this scene Reed had participated in a brief sequence in the vicinity of the United Nations building where his team of soldiers had been shown to apprehend the Iraqi insurgent who had shot at the car containing the bomb. The scene is one of two times the film will show Iraqi prisoners being mistreated, as a medic informs Reed that the injury the man has sustained is survivable, only for the Colonel to inform him in a deadpan fashion, 'He's *not* gonna make it'. The line delivery by Morse is offhand and suitably ambiguous, but the implication is that the man is to be refused treatment and perhaps even killed. As the Colonel strides off shots can be heard in the background, the inference being that the Iraqi was murdered, something which is confirmed in Boal's script with the line 'We HEAR TWO SHOTS, killing the sniper' (2013: 35). It was perhaps this scene which caused the Department of Defense to refuse to support the film as indicated by Lt. Col. J. Todd Breasseale (see Barnes, Parker and Horn, 2010). It might be relevant to note here that this scene of what would be described as a war crime is presented ambiguously, off screen and would perhaps have been missed by many in the audience, a stark contrast to the transgressions of the Iraqi insurgents which are not just portrayed but lingered on and even accentuated by the cinematic devices the film employs, leaving the audience with no doubt of the morality of the war that *The Hurt Locker* places on the screen even when the law is transgressed by American soldiers.

Figure 12

By now, only approximately forty minutes into the film, we have seen
enough of James to begin to understand how he is being framed by
Bigelow through Boal's writing, Ackroyd's cinematography and Renner's
performance, which saw the actor nominated for an Academy Award
and win several other major awards in the period (including Boston Film
Critics, Chicago Film Critics, National Board of Review). How James and
his behaviour is received by the audience is absolutely integral to how
they understand the film. Are we to see him as a reckless, damaged and
dangerous man who displays symptoms of PTSD? Or as an archetypal
movie maverick who does not abide by the rules but stays alive (unlike
Thompson) and gets results (eight hundred and seventy-three of them),
a type with a rich history of antecedents in the genre, in characters like
Lt. Pete 'Maverick' Mitchell (Tom Cruise) from *Top Gun* or Staff Sergeant
Michael Vronsky (Robert De Niro) from *The Deer Hunter*. Moreover,
perhaps the key question for audiences is whether his unconventional
behaviour is endorsed or criticised by *The Hurt Locker*. This, like
many other aspects of the film, has proved divisive. Is it true that, as
Richard Corliss suggested, 'the army needs guys like James' (2008)?
Is he 'basically insane' (Guy Marot, qtd. in Barnett, 2009)? Or is he a
'desensitized, alienated protagonist' (Bennett and Bülent, 2011: 166)? A
synthesisation of these three understandings of James was offered by Ian
Nathan who wrote that he should be regarded as a 'hero/villain/fuck-up
hybrid' (2009). Joshua Clover might have been right to describe him as
'not a little Nietzchean'' (2009: 9) but the term most often returned to in
reviews was that evocative word 'cowboy', which was used to describe
both him *and* his actions, and used as both a noun and an adjective. For
Weitzman he was 'a cowboy with an apparent death wish' (2009), for David
Edelstein a 'Zen cowboy' (2009), for Bob Mondello a 'showboating cowboy'

(2009), for Liza Schwarzbaum someone who 'operates with the swagger of a hothead in a job that depends on cool. That cowboy attitude' (2009). Amy Taubin asked the question, which the film does of its audience, 'Is he a cowboy, so addicted to his adrenaline rush that he's heedless of danger to himself and the men in his unit? Or is he, by virtue of his experience and talents—he says he has disarmed 878 IEDs—simply better than Sanborn or Eldridge at estimating acceptable risk and getting the job done?' (2009: 34). With its rich set of associations not only to the Western genre, but also to the formations of masculinity throughout the twentieth century and into the twenty-first, the cowboy image is evoked throughout the film explicitly and implicitly on a number of occasions: from the Mexican standoff with the taxi driver in the streets of Baghdad and a later sniper duel in the desert, to lines of dialogue like Sanborn's 'Happy trails' and James' own 'I don't know, Sam, I'll tell you when I'm standing over it, cowboy!'

While the Western genre has largely retreated from our cinema and TV screens (with some notable exceptions), the west and the frontier still remain a culturally resonant motif for aspects of American ideology and identity. As Geoff King commented, 'The traditional generic western may be in a state of near terminal decline, but many aspects of the mythic or ideological narrative that animated it remain alive and well in Hollywood' (2000: 2). The genre was alluded to frequently in the period in films like *Taken* (2008), *War of the Worlds* (2005), *Iron Man* (2008), *Logan* (2017) and specifically in the Iraq war film *American Sniper* which has one of its characters greet the eponymous sniper of its title, Chris Kyle (Bradley Cooper), with the line 'Welcome to Fallujah, the new Wild West of the old Middle East'. It is worth commenting that, for the most part, it is not just *any* cowboy that William James is being compared to, but rather a very particular cowboy, the iconic figure of John Wayne, which several commentators specifically turned to. Nochimson stated, 'While Wayne set the testosterone standard in playing characters who lived to fight, his guys also found time to love women... But Will [James], with his Wayne-ian steely gaze, his laconic ease at the portals of death, and his patented hero saunter, loves "just one thing", as he tells his baby boy before leaving him, maybe forever, to return to the killing fields of Iraq. And it isn't women or kids' (2010). Mondello said it is 'the first war movie in a while that feels as if it could have starred John Wayne' (2009), and in an article entitled 'Waiting for John Wayne' describing *The Hurt Locker, The*

Economist suggested 'Perhaps the return of John Wayne is what people have been waiting for' (2008). The 'people' that this is referring to included writers like Peggy Noonan and Kim DuToit, two of many who, in the wake of 9/11, cried out for a return of a more traditional type of masculinity and a man ready and able to protect his family from harm. Peggy Noonan in her October 2001 article 'Welcome Back, Duke. From the ashes of Sept. 11 arise the manly virtues' lamented the loss of this traditional brand of masculinity, which she saw embodied in John Wayne. The kind of men who

> push things and pull things and haul things and build things, men who charge up the stairs in a hundred pounds of gear and tell everyone else where to go to be safe. Men who are welders, who do construction, men who are cops and firemen. They are all of them, one way or another, the men who put the fire out, the men who are digging the rubble out, and the men who will build whatever takes its place.

However, Noonan saw the spirit of John Wayne returning after 9/11: 'But now I think... he's back. I think he returned on Sept. 11. I think he ran up the stairs, threw the kid over his back like a sack of potatoes, came back down and shovelled rubble. I think he's in Afghanistan now, saying, with his slow swagger and simmering silence, "Yer in a whole lotta trouble now, Osama-boy"' (2001). Noonan's article was certainly part of a sustained backlash against the prevailing image of the caring, sharing, sensitive 1990s male characterised by the emergence of stars like Brad Pitt, Matt Damon and Johnny Depp, a far cry from the muscled, hyper-masculine heroes which defined the 1980s which Susan Jeffords considered emblematic of US self-image in her definitive *Hard Bodies: Hollywood Masculinity in the Reagan Era* (1994). Jeffords wrote: 'The depiction of the indefatigable, muscular and invincible masculine body became the lynchpin of the Reagan imaginary; this hardened male form became an emblem not only for the Reagan Presidency but for its ideologies and economies as well' (1994: 25). The 2000s did see these hard-bodies return in Sylvester Stallone (again), Chris Hemsworth and Dwayne 'The Rock' Johnson, but in ways more vulnerable and complicated than they had been presented previously. The character of James then is an interesting articulation of this in *a single body* as were several figures associated with the action genre in this era, from Jason Bourne to Jack Bauer and James Bond. While Janet S. Robinson describes James as having a 'hard-muscled body' (2014: 162) there is much more to him than that: he is emphatically masculine in the traditional sense but at the same time traumatised and troubled, what Francis Pheasant-Kelly called a 'wounded hero' the likes of which became so prominent in post-9/11 cinema (2013: 144). Bigelow described him as 'the man who walks down that street in the direction that everyone else is running from' but also someone aware of his own 'hubris and recklessness' (qtd. in Horton, 2013: 151).

The film does offer more than William James as an example of masculinity, although it is to him as the protagonist the film (and this book) most often returns to. He is placed in juxtaposition to several other men in the film like the already deceased Thompson, but also Eldridge, Sanborn, Reed, Cambridge and of course the Iraqi insurgents, most of whom go unnamed. The war film has been intimately connected to representations of masculinity in its rich history and, as Tasker and Atakev have observed, the genre functions as a 'crucial site for ideas about masculinity, about what it is to be a man' (2010: 58). One might argue that we are not asked to consider Eldridge or Cambridge as an appropriately suitable masculine role model, as even though he is sympathetic Eldridge is shown to be not man enough to fight the war effectively as he continuously complains about their circumstances, plays video games, visits the camp psychologist Cambridge and is content to let Sanborn and James take the lead on their missions. Nor are we asked to consider Dr Cambridge as an appropriate role model. He is a man who instructs people how to deal with their trauma but has never participated in the war in any meaningful way himself and even his name marks him out as an ineffective intellectual the likes of which the war film has historically been dismissive of. When Cambridge goes out with the EOD on a mission, one suspects to prove to himself as much as the men around him that he is a 'real' man, he is shown as too friendly, naive and unguarded outside the safety of his office which is secure within the protective confines of Camp Victory. Asking a group of Iraqis to move their belongings from a dangerous area he pleads with them, 'That's very nice. It's a little unsafe today. So maybe – I don't know – I'm thinking, maybe we should move?' The group finally move leaving behind only an innocuous looking sack which then detonates as the film shows us again and again that *every single Iraqi* is a potential terrorist and murderer. There is nothing left of Cambridge after except for his helmet, as the film shows what happens if one is too friendly with the indigenous people of Iraq. If Iraq is a new millennial frontier, Eldridge and Cambridge are certainly portrayed by Bigelow and Boal as being not man enough to tame it. The only viable alternative that the film offers to James is the level-headed professionalism of Sanborn and the two of them conduct something of a battle for alpha male status within the unit in which some have observed both a racial and even a sexual dimension (see Whitsitt, 2010). For much of the film, even though James is the primary protagonist, Sanborn too is a compelling presence, but the outcome of their interaction is never really in doubt as, rightly or wrongly, *The Hurt Locker* belongs to James. One of the film's most prominently used taglines was 'You don't have to be a hero to do this job. But it helps', a line which undoubtedly refers to him and him alone. The cinematic language and narrative choices lead us towards understanding James as a masculine hero and a decisive man of action the likes of which American film and culture has lauded for more than a century and one that we might admire as Colonel Reed does. The cinematic devices that we have already charted and explored in this book, those that many have connected to Realism, verisimilitude and documentary, in actual fact participate in this process, which Lisa Purse suggests is able to 'mythologise his bravery' (2011: 165). During both bomb encounters we have interrogated so far – the 'daisy chain' bomb on their first day together and the car bomb at the United Nations building – the cinematography and *mise-en-scène* accentuates his bravery and his command of the situation. From simplistic devices such as low angle shots looking up at him so he appears prominent and powerful in the frame while others, including Sanborn and Eldridge, scurry around in a state of panic and discombobulation, to shots of him emerging heroically out of smoke, they all push us towards an 'alignment with and admiration for someone whose compulsion to embrace danger might have registered as alienating in another film' (Purse, 2011: 165). James is the one who never looks confused or scared. In the first mission we are shown American soldiers huddled together in the backyard of an Iraqi house with no idea what to do, their powerlessness embodied in the tiny flags they wave around the corner. When James arrives it is he who tells them 'Keep your boys back... you did good', and he does not want to speak to the Iraqi informant that located the device in the vicinity of the UN building, merely offering 'I'll take care of it'. James is the one who the script provides with 'cool' things to say and he is not far removed from the brooding heroes who have occupied the action genre for decades, those icons of masculinity who have served as an apex of what we are asked to regard as appropriate, even idealised gender behaviour, examples of which have populated some of Kathryn Bigelow's films, such as Captain Mikhail Polenin (Liam Neeson) and Captain Alexei Vostrikov (Harrison Ford) in *K-19: The Widowmaker* (2002), Bodhi (Patrick Swayze) and Johnny Utah (Keanu Reeves) in *Point Break* (1991), and Dan (Jason Clarke) and Patrick (Joel Edgerton) from *Zero Dark Thirty*.

Figure 13

Figure 14

For film scholars and other interested parties, James' character was provided with an additional layer of meaning in the year after the film was released in the light of the court case brought against *The Hurt Locker* by Master Sergeant Jeffrey Sarver, which argued that the film was based on Sarver's own experiences in Iraq and that the portrayal of James as a 'reckless, gung-ho war addict who has a morbid fascination with death' (qtd. in Jeffrey S. Sarver v. The Hurt Locker LLC et al, UNITED STATES DISTRICT COURT DISTRICT OF NEW JERSEY, n.d.s, 15) had done 'injury and damage' to Sarver's reputation (ibid.). While extra-textual analysis of cases like these is not always useful in terms of an understanding of films,

Sarver's suit against *The Hurt Locker* reveals some pertinent perspectives on the film's approach to the character. Mark Boal was indeed embedded with Sarver's unit in Iraq for more than thirty days in 2004, an experience which resulted in the article 'The Man in the Bomb Suit', the title referring to Sarver himself, published in *Playboy* in August/September 2005.[4] Boal vociferously defended himself against these accusations stating that 'the film is a work of fiction inspired by many people's stories' (qtd. in Hinds, 2010) and that the character of James and the narrative of *The Hurt Locker* was the result of interviewing more than a hundred people. He stated that he 'reshuffled everything I learned in a way that would be authentic, but would also make for a dramatic story' (qtd. in Woodall, 2010). The following year the suit was rejected and Sarver was ordered to pay more than $180,000 in attorney fees.[5] Outside of the legal parameters of the case it is clear to see from even a cursory reading of 'The Man in the Bomb Suit' that there is indeed a significant amount of Sarver in William James and enough to see why Sarver believed the character was based on his life and experiences. In the article Sarver is described by Boal as working 'freestyle' and 'off the book' just as James does (2005: 74) and that he keeps 'recovered bomb parts in a box by his bed' (2005: 151) as James is shown to do. In the article Sarver has thirty days left in his deployment, just like James, and even a 'nerdy' partner with 'round steel-framed glasses that give him a rather bookish appearance' (2005: 73) who resembles the characterisation of Eldridge. It is clear James loves what he does and is inescapably drawn to his profession and so does Sarver, who is even more emphatic. Boal quotes him as saying: 'This is great. I love this place. If I keep going, I will have racked up more IEDs and disarmed more bombs than any man in the history of this war' (2005: 73). The experiential approach to the film which we have observed is even anticipated by comments made by Sarver himself who remarks, 'Everything shuts down except you and the device. I can hear myself breathing' (2005: 151). The article also contains a scene with a Colonel that is almost exactly the same as that in the film in the aftermath of the car bomb located in the vicinity of the UN building. The Colonel, who remains unnamed in the article, comments 'Look at that hero. America's finest. That is some good shit. Check that shit out – all right, good job' (ibid.). The only difference in this scene is that the real-life Sarver tells the Colonel that he has dismantled one-hundred and twenty bombs, not the eight-hundred and seventy-three that James states in the film. Boal and

Bigelow choose to make the figure *seven times higher* than the real figure from the article, quite an adjustment for a film about which its writer argued that was designed to be 'lifelike and the whole movie experience to feel tense and authentic' (qtd. in Weintraub, 2009) and whose director suggested 'I don't need to make what they're doing more dramatic' (qtd. in Horton, 2013: 151).[6]

References

1.   The description of Sanborn in the script does not entirely correspond to how the character comes across in the finished film which describes the character as 'a type-A jock, high school football star, cocky, outgoing, ready with a smile and quick with a joke... or, if you prefer, a jab to the chin. Think Muhammad Ali with a rifle' (Boal 2013: 2).

2.   These descriptions do not end there: Markert said the film gives off 'a strong documentary feel' (2011: 244) and Polan that it uses 'hand-held camera, extreme close-up, and a general jitteriness to suggest an in-your-face immediacy' (2012: 232).

3.   The lyrics from 'Khyber Pass' include the lines 'Where's Bin Laden? Where's Bin Laden? He's probably runnin', Probably hidin', Some say he's livin' at the Khyber Pass, Others say he's at the Bush's ranch'.

4.   One of Boal's other *Playboy* articles, 'Death and Dishonour', the source for the film *In the Valley of Elah*, was also involved in a law suit

5.   With a somewhat metatextual sense of irony Sarver's lawyer, Fieger, informed reporters that 'The caveat in the movie that the movie is fictional and all the characters portrayed in the movie are fictional is a fictional statement in and of itself' (qtd. in Hinds 2010).

6.   The similarities and differences between the article and the film are covered in Robert Alpert's '*The Hurt Locker* litigation: an adult's story' (2012). Guy Marot, a bomb disposal expert with fifteen years' experience, said of this number and James' process: 'He's supposed to have dealt with some 870 devices, which is completely unbelievable – it would mean dealing with three improvised explosive devices a day – and he just rocks up near a device and puts on a bomb suit. There's none of the usual military procedure: no planned operation, no isolation, no robots. At one point he is shown pulling five or six 155mm rounds out of the ground, each of those weighs 44kg, and he's wearing a 40-50kg bomb suit as well. The fundamental stupidity is just staggering' (qtd. in Barnett 2009).

Chapter 3: Interpreting The Politics of *The Hurt Locker*

> Pro-war viewers can see a portrait of a sure-footed soldier saving
> the day over and over again, if they like. Anti-war folks can fill in their
> own narrative of imperial hubris and confusion in the scenes where
> James takes an ill-advised trip away from his base. Both readings are
> defensible...
> Seth Colter Walls, 'The Hollowness of *The Hurt Locker*' (*Newsweek*, 21
> January 2010)

'You're what this is all about...': Beckham the 'base rat' and the body bomb

After the United Nations bomb incident described in the previous section,
James, Eldridge and Sanborn drunkenly play fight and bond in a brief yet
emotionally and racially charged scene back at Camp Victory which ends
with Sanborn asking James 'Do you think I got what it takes to put on the
suit?' and James replying '*Hell*, no'. James does not explicitly articulate
what he perceives Sanborn is lacking, but the implication is that he is *just
not man enough* for the job. The film by then has developed a pattern
of alternating bomb defusal missions with time on the base, allowing
the characters to be developed and their relationships deepened. These
scenes also show the friendly rapport between James and a young Iraqi
boy who sells bootleg DVDs on a stall inside Camp Victory who introduces
himself as Beckham (Christopher Sayegh) and never offers his real Arabic
name. The boy is, without a doubt, the closest the film comes to having
an Iraqi characterisation and he is one of just a few Iraqi characters to
be named in the film's diegesis and in the credits. The majority of the
Iraqi characters (if they are placed in the credits at all) are listed by their
profession or appearance like 'Iraqi Translator', 'Butcher', 'Insurgent
Sniper', 'Iraqi Police Captain' and 'Black Suit man', in what might be
read as a gesture symptomatic of the film's refusal to acknowledge the
lives of others. The interactions between James and Beckham, who is
described as a 'base rat' by Eldridge and a 'street savvy punk' in the script
(2013: 30), produce the film's most intimate, but also some of its most
disturbing moments. As we have seen, James is repeatedly shown as
being uncomfortable around people, but it is Beckham he has the closest
connection to of all the characters featured in the narrative, including
even his own family when he returns to America at the end of the film.
They are shown laughing and joking together and playing football, and

James even hugs the boy who expresses his admiration for the work the EOD does in broken English in a way that recalls Colonel Reed's outside the United Nations building from earlier: 'It fun no? It's cool, it's gangster?' James replies with one of the rare acknowledgements of how he feels about his profession, 'Yeah... I think so'. The relationship is certainly an odd one and James, in a strange aside, threatens to 'chop off your [Beckham's] goddamn head with a dull knife' if the next DVD the boy supplies him with is not a perfect copy, before he quickly reveals that he is joking. Although, given what seems to happen to Beckham later in the film the exchange is a doubly uncomfortable one.

Figure 15

Children often have a specific function in the war film, not just as characters within the diegesis but also, at times, symbolically representative of all that any given conflict is being fought for in the first place. For example, in John Wayne's contentious *The Green Berets* (1968), a film which rewrites the complicated geo-politics of the war in Vietnam into something that resembles the simplistic moral binarisms of a Classical Hollywood Western, Wayne's Colonel Mike Kirby tells a little Vietnamese boy '*You're* what this is all about'. As Gary Wills wrote about *The Green Berets* 'People who did not want to know about the actual Vietnam War could feel that the national unity and resolve of World War II might turn around this strange new conflict in the far-off jungles of the East. Wayne was fighting World War II again, the only way he ever did, in make-believe; and that make-believe was a memory of American greatness that many still wanted to live by' (1997: 223). It might be argued that films like *The Hurt Locker* and *American Sniper* perform a very similar cultural role for the divisive conflicts in Iraq and Afghanistan, whether their creators intended them to or not. Films about the wars in

Iraq and Afghanistan rarely use children as simplistically as in *The Green Berets*, but given the potency of their image they are still present. In *In the Valley of Elah* the event which prompts the soldier Mike Deerfield's PTSD is the fact that he had run over an Iraqi child in his Humvee; in *Stop-Loss* US Army Staff Sergeant Brandon King (Ryan Phillippe) throws a grenade into a room which he thinks is full of insurgents only to find that he has killed a group of children; in the opening scenes of *American Sniper* Chris Kyle is shown to be *forced* to kill an Iraqi child carrying a grenade. The film shows how deeply reluctant Kyle is to pull the trigger, but that he is *right to shoot* and in doing so saves the lives of many of his comrades. The scene is constructed in such a way that we do not question whether his actions were the right thing to do, or what would motivate an Iraqi family to involve their child in the war, but only what kind of an evil parent would tell their child to do such a thing?

James and his team are called out on the day the film identifies as being the sixteenth day left in their rotation on what Eldridge describes it as 'a pretty standard mission. We're just here to pick up some ordnance', but it turns out to be much more than that. When they arrive at the location it is revealed to have once been a school, but is no longer. As the team carefully look around it is clear that the insurgents must have left just moments before as a cigarette is still burning and a kettle is still on the boil, adding to the imminent and ever-present sense of threat the film has dwelled on since its opening moments. As usual it is James who is shown to be both the bravest and the most accomplished soldier among them, Sanborn treads on glass and the loud cracks echo through the building which could have alerted the enemy to their position. The scene employs the Realist aesthetic strategies we have described in the book so far, but there is something slightly different about the way this sequence is presented which gives it an at times vaguely expressionistic quality. Instead of only books and desks in the school, they find extensive bomb making equipment and resources, much of which is shown to be American in origin, and what the script rather glibly describes as 'Santa's bomb making factory' (2013: 79). It is there that the team also finds the dead body of a child on a table. James, with the preternatural skill he is often shown to have throughout the film, notices something different about the body and discovers that the insurgents have placed explosives inside the corpse, turning it into an IED: one of many ways the film asks us to understand the difference between the noble and heroic Americans and the cruel and even demonic Iraqi insurgents. James is convinced it is the boy Beckham, the only human being the film has shown him having a connection to, but Sanborn and Eldridge are not sure, with the African American Sanborn offering the loaded line 'they all look alike to me'. The irony lingers, even though it is unclear whether Boal or director Bigelow is aware of it or not. At this point in the film it is not entirely clear whether the dead boy on the table is Beckham, but later it will categorically reveal that it is *not* when he shows up alive and well back at the base. Boal confirmed this in interview that 'The kid on the table is not Beckham, although it looks like him. Sanborn and Eldridge knows it is not the same kid, but they don't realize how much it is affecting James' (qtd. in Rubin, 2011: 275). Despite this diegetic and non-diegetic clarification the uncertainty lingered for some writers, even Robert Burgoyne, who wrote

The scene reaches a heightened quality of visceral intensity as James decides to dismantle the bomb inside Beckham's abdomen, an act that puts into a single frame the imagery of bomb defusing, with its wires, leads and secret triggers, and the imagery of surgery, the manipulation of organs, vessels and flesh. James' delicate and intricate work, his skill with his hands, takes on a new meaning, as the almost tender act of working on Beckham's body brings into relief the somatic focus of the war film, its concentrated body imagery, and its baseline of visceral experience. Filmed in extreme close-up, the sound track dominated by James' breathing and the buzzing of the occasional fly, the sequence culminates in James lifting the explosive from Beckham's chest cavity. He then wraps the body in a white sheet, and carries it from the building. James' rescue of Beckham's body can easily be read as pathological, and the scene itself as an ideologically loaded manipulation of audience emotion, depicting grotesque body trauma in order to make a flagrant political point about the villainy of the insurgency in Iraq. (2012: 16-17)

James is powerfully affected by the scene and it is unclear as to exactly why, as he has shown himself largely calm, collected and seemingly unaffected by the dangers of the war around him throughout the film. It is certainly the most emotion he shows across the film's two hour running time. Boal's script explains that *The war has finally reached him* (2013: 81, italics in original). The purpose of the scene is ambiguously presented.

Is it to finally show that the war has got through to James? Does it make James think of his own son back in America? Does it make him realise that if he lets his guard down this is what happens? Does it underscore the essential inhumanity of the terrorist insurgents in troublingly simplistic ways, while at the same time showing James and his team as more human than any Iraqi the film cares to place in front of its camera? Is it, like Burgoyne, suggests 'a stark reminder of the barbarism of war' (2012: 17)? The scene is troubling for these reasons and more and, as Peebles asserts, it 'takes the trope of the dead child to a new extreme' (2011: 168). It is hard to deny its affective power and the skilfulness with which it is filmed and played by the performers, but its motivation and what it informs audiences about the war in Iraq is problematic. James brings the body outside covered in a sheet after refusing to allow the team to detonate the building with him in it. This shot is artfully filmed and certainly departs from a Realist aesthetic as for a few seconds the shot is blurry, but as James, cradling the boy's body walks down the corridor, he walks into focus. The fact that there is no recorded evidence of such a scheme ever being used in Iraq reveals more about the film's desire to imagine monstrosities which continue to demonise Iraqi insurgents whilst at the same time glorifying James' singular humanity and heroism, his status as an American hero, who *feels* and *understands* things more than everyone around him. Furthermore, Sanborn's line to Eldridge, 'You ever seen a body bomb before?', has encoded within it the implication that *he* has, the suggestion being that this one is not the first, nor will it be the last. One might compare this fictionalisation to the much-criticised Russian roulette sequence from *The Deer Hunter*. It was reported that on one of its early screenings at the Berlin Film Festival in 1979, not only did representatives of the Soviet Union walk out but also those from Cuba, East Germany and many other Eastern European countries, in protest at what it suggested about America's ideological enemies. The war film plays a central role in how audiences are encouraged to view those on the other side of this ideological divide, as the former soldier Stan Goff wrote: 'When I was in Vietnam, we were taught to refer to the Vietnamese as gooks. This name calling is always a part of any military aggression because soldiers have to be brought along in their dehumanization of those they are obliged by conditions and ignorance to abuse, dominate, and kill. Social psychologists tell us that we are overcoming "cognitive dissonance" when we do that' (2004: 147). Films, then, can perpetuate or challenge these stereotypes in how they represent the Other on the screen, regardless of the conflict that they represent and whether they are from the distant past or the present. It is clear to see that *The Hurt Locker* has made very particular choices in how it has decided to portray the Iraqis, and that as well as these choices directing the way the film is perceived by audiences, they can even come to influence the way the actual conflict itself comes to be remembered.

Figure 16

Figure 17

The scene would be potent enough were its significance to end here, but later in the film back at Camp Victory James sees Beckham alive and well playing football in what is perhaps the film's most ambiguous moment, revealing that he was *wrong* and the dead child was not Beckham at all. What are audiences to take from his reappearance? Does it alter our experience with the body bomb scene the way it must have with James? It too has been interpreted in many ways by many commentators: Robinson offers the idea that 'The mis-identification of the body as Beckham underscores the contradictions at stake in terrorist violence' (2014: 163); Joshua Clover gives us 'the boy has served his purpose, a mute justification for another visit to the firefight' (2009: 9); Peebles suggests

'James ignores him, and whatever his feelings are – frustration, shame, sadness – he hides them behind a blank stare' (2011: 169). Westwell states that 'this scene seems designed to symbolize the barbarity and inscrutability of the enemy, as well as to posit Iraq as the home of a civil struggle (with Iraqi killing Iraqi) in which America has a role only as an unwitting and well-intentioned catalyst' (2013: 396). The script reads: 'James stops. He stares. What can he say? The boy is fine... Unable to face the kid and unwilling to explain, James turns and stiffly gets into the Humvee' (2013: 99). Why have Bigelow and Boal shown James to be mistaken and what can it mean for the film's representation of the Iraqi Other? Robert Kolker rather generously reads the boy reappearing as a 'gesture to the futility of passion in this horrendous war' (2011: 301); however, Sanborn's earlier comment – that 'they all look the same' – lingers. It is in this scene of misrecognition that the ideological contradictions and ruptures of the film's depiction of a 'Good War' force their way to the surface. To misrecognise the Other is to deny his/her humanity, and for James to acknowledge that Beckham is alive and that the dead boy was someone else would be to concede that his judgement is flawed and that indeed 'they all look the same' for him also. James is confronted with a superlative example of his own cognitive dissonance, but it is too difficult for him to process. His only reaction can be to refuse to acknowledge it and to turn his head the other way.

The Politics of Apoliticism: *The Hurt Locker* as 'embedded' film-making

Rasheed passes the bridal shop
on a bicycle, with Sefa beside him,
and just before the air ruckles and breaks
he glimpses the sidewalk reflections
in the storefront glass, men and women
walking and talking, or not, an instant
of clarity, just before each of them shatters
under the detonation's wave,
as if even the idea of them were being
destroyed, stripped of form,
the blast tearing into the manikins
who stood as though husband and wife
a moment before, who cannot touch

one another, who cannot kiss,
who now lie together in glass and debris,
holding one another in their half-armed embrace,
calling this love, if this is all there will ever be.

'2000 lbs' by Brian Turner in *Here, Bullet* (2007: 42-43).

Brian Turner's collection of poetry *Here, Bullet* (2007) offers a remarkable account of the author's time in the United States Army during his deployment in Iraq from 2003, not too long before Kathryn Bigelow's *The Hurt Locker* is set. His poems 'The Hurt Locker', '2000lbs', 'Tigris River Blues' and 'What Every Soldier Should Know' have seen him described as a 'descendent' of Wilfred Owen and David Jones (see Forché, n.d.s) with texts so able to articulate the experiences of those who fought in the war that it was suggested he had 'picked up where Wilfred Owen and Keith Douglas left off' (Crown, 2010). However, in the first decade of the new millennium there is so little coverage of poetry in the news media that very rarely do any poets or their work ever become a part of popular culture. This is a far cry from the First World War (1914-18) when the likes of Wilfred Owen, Siegfried Sassoon, Alfred Lichtenstein and August Stramm emerged as key chroniclers of the conflict, some of whom were read by millions at the time and their work now regarded as resonant cultural artefacts which provide an insight into the horrors of a war which saw tens of millions of dead and wounded over the course of four years. Of course, as we have seen, it is now the cinema, and to a lesser extent television, which defines how conflicts come to be viewed in the cultural imagination. Turner's work, as revealed in the single stanza from the poem '2000lbs' quoted from above does what this book has suggested films about the wars in Iraq and Afghanistan have been unwilling or unable to do in the years since Sidney J. Furie's *American Soldiers: A Day in Iraq* (2005); that is, provide perspectives other than that of the US soldiers that are the protagonists in films about the war. *The Hurt Locker*, like the vast majority of American films about the 9/11 wars, represents the American experience of Iraq through a range of narrative and cinematic devices in dramas which, it should be repeated, have every right to be told by their creators in any way they see fit. But at the same time, it is imperative that we acknowledge that these decisions do not result in apolitical texts, but rather films which are entirely immersed in the ideological currents of their era.

One might regard these films as being similar to reports produced by embedded journalists during the wars in Iraq and Afghanistan. While the process of embedded journalism was expected to generate a first-hand, boots on the ground depiction of the conflict from a diverse range of perspectives, in actual fact the result was that it

> failed to deliver on its promise to provide different angles of perception.
> First, the practice has significantly limited the scope and outlook
> of news in space and time, often reducing it to the individual unit,
> while neglecting the larger social and political context, including the
> perspectives of other relevant actors, such as victims, enemies and
> other people affected by the war. Second, many journalists or editors
> consciously presented a sanitized version of the war, as it was deemed
> 'indecent' or 'in bad taste' to show domestic audiences images of
> civilian casualties, American casualties or other gruesome scenes of
> war. Embedded journalists sometimes also toned down the culture
> of martial masculinity, which in turn made it easier for audiences to
> identify or even develop an affective relationship with the soldiers. (Van
> Munster, 2015: 117)

Van Munster's cogent summary of the impact of embedded journalism is supported by a diverse range of studies both analytical and empirical (see Katovsky and Carlson, 2003; Barkawi, 2005) and it is clear to see the elements described are just as applicable to not only news reports made about the wars in Iraq and Afghanistan but also fiction films, many of which are based on autobiographies, memoirs or first-hand accounts of the war. Thus, we can see this present in films like *Lone Survivor* (film 2013, book 2007) based on the book by Marcus Lutrell (and Patrick Robinson) which depicts Operation Red Wing in Afghanistan in 2005, *American Sniper* (film 2014, book 2012) the book by Chris Kyle (and Scott McEwen), and perhaps most significantly *Zero Dark Thirty*, the film about the pursuit and eventual assassination of Osama Bin Laden, which was also directed by Kathryn Bigelow and scripted by Mark Boal. On the relationship between the film and governmental institutions of the United States, Peter Maas argued that *Zero Dark Thirty* 'represents a troubling new frontier of government-embedded filmmaking' (2013). Maas' assertion is that the high levels of access to the CIA that Bigelow and Boal received while preparing the project distorted their perspective on the events and thus correspondingly influenced the shape of the film (see

Child, 2013; McSweeney, 2014; Westwell, 2014). *The Hurt Locker* provides us with another pertinent example of this phenomenon as Mark Boal was *literally* an embedded journalist during the conflict, an experience which resulted in the *Playboy* article 'The Man with the Bomb Suit' and then, a few years later, the film itself. One might argue that as audiences it is we that have been embedded into films about the wars in Iraq and Afghanistan, which very rarely feature prominent characters of Iraqi and Afghanistan origin, with some rare exceptions, and certainly do not tell the stories of the indigenous peoples of the region.

The Hurt Locker, like *Lone Survivor*, *American Sniper* and the vast majority of American films about the wars in Iraq and Afghanistan marginalises, distorts and erases the Iraqi and Afghanistani experiences of the war, removing its uncomfortable and unpalatable aspects in favour of a reification of the master narrative of the conflict. In doing this, these films refuse to represent what Judith Butler described as the 'precarious lives' of non-western people in her *Precarious Life: The Powers of Mourning and Violence* (2004). *The Hurt Locker* is a film which portrays almost every Iraqi citizen, man, woman and child as a threat to the soldiers. These Iraqis are frequently viewed through the rifle sights of the Americans who are at the centre of the film and this act itself is portrayed as entirely necessary and appropriate in narratives that have refused a process of reverse focalisation and by extension moral equivalence. The tortuous logic that these films embrace is well hidden from the audience in affective acts of *legerdemain*: like how, in *American Sniper*, Chris Kyle is shown to be a hero even though he shoots and kills an Iraqi child, and that being a sniper in a war of occupation can be a defensive and heroic act, but an enemy sniper is a despicable coward, and that the true victim of the war is not the hundreds and thousands of wounded, dead and displaced civilians, but the American soldier himself. There are numerous comparable moments in *The Hurt Locker*, perhaps even too many to explore: whether it is the failure of the film to provide Iraqis a legitimate voice against occupation, as all those who oppose America's presence are violent insurgents, or Sanborn's incredulity at the UN building when those he is pointing his loaded gun at do not wave back at him in a gesture of friendship.

It is useful for a moment to pause to see how some of these Iraqi characters are described in Boal's original script, if they are described at all, in yet another indication of how little interest the film has in their perspective. No description is offered of the Iraqi sergeant who informs James about the location of the car bomb at the UN building (2013: 34), or the insurgent sniper on the rooftops who is later murdered on the orders of Colonel Reed in the same scene (33), the numerous snipers in the desert duel, the Iraqi peasants who interact with Dr. Cambridge (80), or the older Iraqi man who sells DVDs on the camp who James takes hostage (86) in a scene we will explore in more detail later. However, the Butcher, the man who detonates the bomb that kills Thompson is described first as 'furious' (2) and then as 'cantankerous' (5); the taxi driver that engages in the quasi-Mexican standoff with James is described in the script as 'Impossible to discern whether he's simply an annoyed taxi driver—or a Jihadi on a suicide mission' (24); and the man on the minaret at the United Nations building is only described as 'angry' (44). This is a stark contrast to the humanity which is afforded to the American characters in the film, flawed or otherwise: thus Sanborn is 'cocky, outgoing, ready with a smile and quick with a joke' (2); Eldridge is 'impressionable, vulnerable, yet quite capable of showing surprising backbone' (4); James is 'fit and good-looking, one of the lucky ones' (15); and even Colonel Reed, who, with just a few minutes of screen time, is described as 'a salty officer... whose uniform shimmers with military bling and Army skill patches' (35).

Our focus, of course, is *The Hurt Locker*, but we could just as easily have compiled such a list for the majority of American films about the wars in Iraq and Afghanistan and have seen a largely similar result. As crude as it may sound, there are more American films which portray the experiences of *dogs* during the wars in Iraq and Afghanistan and their aftermath – films like *Max* (2015) and *Meagan Leavey* (2017) – than there are which focus on the lives of the indigenous peoples of the region. In *The Hurt Locker* each Iraqi functions only as what they can reveal about the Americans who are at the core of the film: the plight of 'Beckham' tells us about James' humanity, the taxi driver about his composure, the sniper at the UN building about his bravery and commitment to saving lives rather than taking them. These decisions, on the surface, might seem arbitrary and not ideologically motivated, but they produce very specific results when repeated in film after film; that is, a prioritisation of the American experience and life above all with the others pushed to the margins, if present at all. We are rarely offered glimpses of the lives of others in these films in the way that the poet Brian Turner offers even in just the single stanza of '2000 lbs.' used as an epigraph to this section where he recounts the explosion of a suicide bomb in Ashur Square in Mosul, and how that single moment impacts on the lives of those caught in the blast: on an Iraqi couple, Rasheed and Sefa, passing by on a bicycle, an American officer, Lt. Jackson, inside a Humvee, an old woman begging with her infant grandson, and even the suicide bomber, who remains unnamed. The humanity contained within these few lines offers more than *The Hurt Locker* is able to do for its depiction of Iraqis in its running time of more than two hours.

One of the most memorable episodes of how the film centralises the experiences of those from the west is an eighteen-minute-long vignette set in the desert which begins with James, Sanborn and Eldridge coming across a squad of British mercenaries stranded due to mechanical problems with their vehicle. It is the second, after the death of the insurgent sniper at the United Nations building, of the two sequences which may have caused the Pentagon to refuse to support the film due to scenes of Iraqi prisoners being mistreated. Their leader, an unnamed character played by Ralph Fiennes gestures towards the two captives that the script describes thus: 'two ENEMY PRISONERS OF WAR (EPWs, or so we assume), shrouded in black hoods, hands bound, are kneeling uncomfortably on the desert floor' (2013: 55). Fiennes is eager to recount the details of his prize with James and indicates that one of them is the 'Nine of Hearts' and the other 'Al Rawi, Jack of Clubs'. The most-wanted military playing cards, officially known as 'personality identification playing cards' were distributed by the US military in order to identify high ranking officials within Saddam Hussein's government and army. Both of the characters named on the screen are not fictional, but real-life individuals: the nine of Hearts was Mizban Khadr Hadi (b. 1938), a general and politician in Ba'athist Iraq and member of the Revolutionary Command Council from 1991 to 2001, reported to have been caught and arrested in Baghdad on 1 May 2003. The Jack of Clubs was Sayf Al-Din Fulayyih Hasan Taha Al-Rawi, Chief of Iraqi Republican Guard, who as of 2017 was unaccounted for (see 'Iraq Most Wanted Fast Facts'). When the mercenaries and the EOD unit come under fire from a group of insurgents in the distance, including more than one sniper, Fiennes appears almost as concerned about his bounty running away than he does about one of his team being shot, before he remembers that the prisoners are worth the same amount of money to him alive or dead – 'half a million quid!' – and shoots them both in the back while laughing as they attempt to flee. But moments later he too is shot and killed rather ignominiously which leads to a tense long-range duel as James and Sanborn, for once working in harmony, take on the Iraqi sniper team. As ever, it is James who is calm and composed and guides his team to victory by the conclusion of the scene.

Figure 18

While it is true that the film refuses to make overtly political statements, like Eldridge's comment about the useless presence of American tanks in Iraq and the poor quality of the cart that the ANDROS remote pulls at the beginning of the film, with even these being fairly muted, its political perspectives are subsumed into its narrative and cinematic choices. Several commentators, in fact the majority of reviewers on the film's release, mistakenly viewed this lack of direct discussion of the geo-political significance and causes of the war as evidence that the film was *apolitical*, that *The Hurt Locker* was a *neutral* account of the conflict which refused to take sides, and furthermore should be praised *for not doing so* as David Denby did with his suggestion that the film reduces 'the war to the existential confrontation of man and deadly threat' allowing it to be enjoyed 'without ambivalence or guilt' (2009). Yet it is important to recognise that choosing not to explicitly portray politics is *not the same at all* as being apolitical. As we have seen on a number of occasions the film is deeply rooted in ideology despite claims by its film-makers and reviewers to the contrary. Whether we consider its refusal to portray Iraqis with any sense of humanity, its depiction of all insurgents as monstrous (even by inventing atrocities) or how it portrays almost all Americans as heroically altruistic, *The Hurt Locker* is an avowedly political film from its first frames to its last in the way that Jean-Louis Comolli and Jean Narboni, writing in *Cahiers du cinema*, argued that 'every film is political, inasmuch as it is determined by the ideology which produces it' (1977: 24-25). Comolli and Narboni adopted a useful classification of Hollywood films into several groups: ranging from those which presented dominant ideology in 'pure unadulterated form' (1977: 5) to others which challenged it in different ways and to various extents. The most interesting and relevant of these categories for discerning whether any given Hollywood film, regardless of its genre, might offer a semblance of counter-hegemonic discourse is their classification of films 'which at first sight seem to belong firmly within the ideology and to be completely under its sway, but which turn out to be so only in an ambiguous manner [...] an internal criticism [...] which cracks the film apart at the seams' (1977: 7). Whether *The Hurt Locker* 'cracks apart at the seams' or not has been a substantial part of what this book has attempted to interrogate.

Many films about the 'War on Terror' attempt something similar to *The Hurt Locker* in their sustained effort to appear apolitical. Paul Greengrass's *United 93* and *World Trade Center* (2006) by Oliver Stone were both praised by reviewers for their apolitical narratives and, on the surface, in a similar way to which we have seen in *The Hurt Locker*, they appear to avoid politics. But Slavoj Žižek was one of a few who challenged these claims when he wrote

> ...both films are restrained from taking a political stance and depicting the wider context of the events. Neither the passengers on United 93 nor the policemen in WTC grasp the full picture [....] The result is that the political message of the two films resides in their abstention from delivering a direct political message. It is the message of an implicit trust in one's government: when under attack, one just has to do one's duty. ('On 9/11, New Yorkers Faced the Fire in the Minds of Men', 2006: 30)

In the case of *The Hurt Locker*, stylistic and narrative choices embrace the Realist aesthetic and seem to support claims of apoliticism, but they are imbued with ideological perspectives, whether the film-makers intend them to be or not.

In the aftermath of the death of Beckham, James returns to the base and decides to do something about it by going AWOL to look for those who murdered the boy. In a provocative and exhilarating five-minute-long scene he takes the Iraqi man who had sold DVDs alongside Beckham in Camp Victory hostage and demands that he be taken to where Beckham lived. The entire episode which follows is certainly the film's most criticised sequence, particularly by veterans of the war who suggested that it was simply implausible that an American soldier would go AWOL out alone into the city at night wearing a hoodie and looking for revenge (see Reickhoff, 2010; Smith, 2010; Hoit, 2010). Iraq War veteran Kate Hoit wrote: 'While I watched that scene I automatically thought, there isn't a soldier in the world who would leave their base and run through Baghdad unless they were trying to commit suicide. I laughed out-loud in the theater — could anyone actually believe this? Bravo Hollywood; that was pure magical bullshit' (2010). Indeed, it is one of the more 'movie-like' moments in the film and it does seem like something out of a Hollywood thriller rather than a documentary (as the film was often compared to), the likes of which Renner went on to feature in after his breakout performance in *The Hurt Locker* made him an international star in such films as *Mission Impossible: Ghost Protocol* (2011), *The Avengers* (2012) and *The Bourne Legacy* (2012) (which is doubly ironic given that Paul Rieckhoff wrote about the scene 'He goes outside the wire in civilian clothes and goes roaming around downtown Baghdad like Jason Bourne' [qtd. in Bowman, 2010]). While the sequence might be improbable, like much of the film it is powerfully affectual, well shot and staged, placing viewers very much in James' shoes for the duration with its cinematography and soundscape skilfully designed. The cinematic techniques employed, many of which we have discussed already, attempt to make us feel James' sense of disorientation through its hand-held and destabilising cinematography. When he arrives at the house where he has been told Beckham *used* to live, he takes out his pistol and goes inside. The audience wonder what he will find? Another bomb-making factory? A base full of heavily armed insurgents? One might argue that the codes and conventions of the genre lead us to expect such a violent confrontation in which James will be tested and once again prove his masculinity as he has done numerous times already throughout the film. But instead he finds a well-furnished, middle-class Iraqi home and a softly spoken Iraqi intellectual who calls himself Professor Nabil (Nabil

Koni). When James tells him 'I'm looking for the people *responsible* for Beckham', a statement that is ambiguously constructed in and of itself, Nabil replies 'You are CIA no? I am very pleased to see CIA in my home.' It is very rare to be offered a view of the Iraqi domestic space in an American war film and instead of the violent scene perhaps James and the audience have anticipated, Nabil welcomes him, an intruder, into his home and offers to converse with him in English, French or Arabic. It is only the professor's wife, understandably shocked and surprised at the appearance of an American soldier, who attacks James with a frying pan which cuts him on the forehead, giving him the worst wound he is shown to receive in the entire film. In this scene, as in the rest of the film, *The Hurt Locker* decides to leave the Arabic untranslated, but what the wife actually yells to her husband is 'Why is this man here?!' and to James she shouts 'Get out!'.[7] The decision whether or not to translate the languages spoken by the enemy and civilians in the war film, regardless of the conflict, is a relevant and important one with considerable impact on viewers. If the language spoken, whether Arabic, Vietnamese, German or any other, is left untranslated it is once again an immersive device, placing us in the shoes of the American soldiers. If it is translated and the American soldiers do not understand *but we do*, this places us in a different position to them in terms of our knowledge of the situation.

Once again it is not clear what audiences are supposed to take from this scene. While on the way to the house James might have been 'roaming around downtown Baghdad like Jason Bourne' his time inside is far from a triumphant consolidation of the revenge he was looking for and the whole episode is shown to have been based on false information which results in confusion and disappointment. Burgoyne suggests that James 'pursues phantom villains' which 'drive the character along a downward spiral that begins to resemble a death wish, as the character takes on a kind of willed abjection' (2012: 17). Westwell argues that, 'Presumably this is intended to reflect the difficulty James faces in trying to make sense of the war... but it also has the effect of casting all Iraqis as inscrutable, masked, and potentially dangerous' (2013: 396). Are we being prompted to question whether James has been conditioned to see Iraqis only as a threat and that he cannot process when they are not? Or is it supposed to humanise Iraqis for James *and* for audiences? Whatever the intention is, James finds no answers in the professor's house and neither do we.

Figure 19

Figure 20

On his return to Camp Victory, which he is only able to do by informing the American soldier at the gate that he had been to a brothel and that he would give the man the address, he is called out straight away on another mission. This time James, Sanborn and Eldridge are tasked with undertaking a post-blast assessment of a suspected suicide attack on an oil tanker in the Green Zone in what will be the last mission the film shows of the three members of the EOD team together. James has had no sleep, is certainly affected emotionally, physically and psychologically by the events of the day and throughout the sequence the film asks us to doubt his actions more than it has at any time before. Arriving at the scene of the explosion the team are confronted with what the script describes as 'a Hieronymus Bosch nightmare of tangled limbs and body parts' (2013: 91). The location is full of victims, all of which seem to be Iraqis, with dead bodies strewn about the bomb site which is only lit up by bright orange fire still burning. The camera follows the team but again its focus is primarily on James who sees women wailing and praying for those they have lost and lingers on the victims themselves and even their missing body parts. If any one scene in *The Hurt Locker* is designed to reveal the horrors of the war in Iraq it is this one. Yet the way it is constructed is not inconsequential: the destroyed tanker would have provided oil for Iraqis given to them by Americans in their altruistic desire to return stability and order to the country which is prevented by the attacks of the insurgents in yet another example of everything the US is shown to be doing there coinciding with the image of the war George W. Bush promulgated and what we might understand to be the 'master narrative' of the wars in Iraq and Afghanistan. Overlooking the devastation James again becomes swept away by the sights of insurgent barbarity, what kind of people would do such a thing? The script suggests that James now 'seems lost in a private war of his own. The insurgents are out there somewhere. Ahab and the Whale' (2013: 94). Yet the film has mythologised him too much for this to come across in the final film. While we are being asked to challenge some of James' perspectives, he is still undeniably and undoubtedly its hero, who has dismantled *every* bomb, seen *every* threat, and saved all of his team mates *every* time he was asked to. Are we now to consider him as unbalanced and dangerous when the film has spent so long ensuring that we identify with him and recognise him as an archetypal movie maverick who might break the rules, but gets the job done, again and again?

Looking out over the destruction James asks his team members, 'What if there was no body? What if it was a remote det? A really good bad guy hides out in the dark, right?' With that he orders Sanborn and Eldridge to leave the perimeter with him looking for the perpetrators of the bombing in the streets of Baghdad late at night in another deviation from protocol and another episode that was heavily criticised by veterans. Sanborn protests and insists that there are US soldiers out there specifically trained for this job, but James will have none of it. They venture out into the darkness where James orders them to 'Split up to flush them out' and as they move through the streets they come across groups of children before both James and Sanborn are shown to hear shots coming from Eldridge's position. When they reach where the sounds came from they discover that Eldridge has been taken by insurgents. While it is James who certainly got them into this mess, it is also him that, as always, gets them out of it and they manage to find Eldridge just before he is driven away, with James killing both men attempting to bundle him into the back of a car. Eldridge is shot in the fracas and it is not entirely clear, although it is implied, that his wounds were caused by James himself. Here we see the paradox which the film offers us. James is its hero but we are asked, on occasion, to consider him as unbalanced: what we are to do with this paradox is up to audiences to decide. In the space of a few hours James has had two unorthodox missions outside the confines of Camp Victory and both have resulted in absolutely nothing: both are set up by Boal and Bigelow with the expectation of heroic acts of catharsis, but deliver only disappointment and injury. James returns back to the base again and enters the shower in his full combat gear, a simplistic trope which encourages the audience to identify with James' emotionally troubled state (see similar scenes in *Casino Royale* [2005] and *Close Encounters of the Third Kind* [1977]). The next day as the wounded Eldridge is being placed in a helicopter in order to be flown back to America his words directed at James have the aforementioned paradox within them: 'Thanks for saving my life, but we didn't have to go out looking for trouble just to get your adrenaline fix!'

Figure 21

References

7.   I would like to thank Abdalla Mohamed Moussa at Solent University for this translation.

Chapter 4: The Reception of *The Hurt Locker*: Anti-War or 'War Porn'?

> Realism has its thrills, too. The insistence on plainness, the absence of stylization, carries over to the performances as well.... '*The Hurt Locker*' is a small classic of tension, bravery, and fear, which will be studied twenty years from now when people want to understand something of what happened to American soldiers in Iraq. If there are moviegoers who are exhausted by the current fashion for relentless fantasy violence, this is the convincingly blunt and forceful movie for them.
> David Denby, *The New Yorker* 29 June 2009

Metaphors, the final mission and the reluctant suicide bomber

As we have seen throughout the course of this book *The Hurt Locker* was one of the most positively reviewed American films in the year it was released and it is certainly the most critically praised film about the wars in Iraq and Afghanistan at the time of writing. Many of the reviews emphasised how realistic it was (see Schwarzbaum, 2009; Turan, 2009; Scott, 2010), its experiential immediacy (Foundas, 2009; Denby, 2009), its contribution to how the war would come to be remembered (Corliss, 2008; LaSalle, 2009) and its status as an apolitical text (Foundas; Denby; Smith, 2009). Many of them were similar to Mick LaSalle's who wrote that *The Hurt Locker* 'has a fullness of understanding that sets it apart. On the day of its release, this one enters the pantheon of great American war films - and puts Kathryn Bigelow into the top tier of American directors.' Yet despite this overwhelming embrace of the film, it did prove problematic for some. Many of those more critical interpretations of the film came to the exact opposite conclusion: thus, while for Liza Schwarzbaum the film was to be understood in the following way, 'This ain't no war videogame, no flashy, cinematic art piece; there's nothing virtual about this reality' (2009), Marilyn Young, who titled her review of the film in *Perspectives on History* 'The Hurt Locker: War as a Video Game' (2009), argued that 'Here, [in *The Hurt Locker*] Americans are the targets of bombs rather than the ones who drop the bombs. No Iraqi civilians are killed by an American hand; the unit shoots only at Iraqis who shoot back; and the Iraqi enemy, rigging the tortured bodies of boys with explosives or locking a possibly unwilling man into a suicide bomb vest, is despicable, inhuman. *The Hurt Locker* is the perfect Iraq war movie, allowing the audience to support the troops without needing to wonder whether they should be fighting there in the first place. It offers no explanations, no apologies and only a thin patina of regret.'

These starkly contrasting differences of opinion can also be found articulated by those who actually served in the armed forces. Veterans like Paul Rieckhoff, Executive Director of the Iraq and Afghanistan Veterans of America (IAVA), Kate Hoit and Richard Allen Smith, were very critical of the film's portrayal of the military for a variety of reasons. Their complaints about the film are varied, some might be regarded as minor and others more substantial: they range from the lack of accuracy concerning the film's uniforms (see Smith, 2010; Hoit, 2010); deviation from standard bomb disposal procedures, about which Rieckhoff commented, 'Very seldom is a guy going to put on a bomb suit and walk down there and try and dismantle something by hand... It just doesn't make sense. For the most part, they're going to use robotics; they're going to use other types of explosives to set off a charge — a controlled charge — next to it. It's really a Hollywood sensationalized version of how EOD operate' (qtd. in Bowman, 2010); the EOD team operating by themselves in the field frequently without military support (Hoit; Smith, 2010), and the recklessness of James' behaviour and how it is not feasible for someone in his position to behave in such a way without facing reprimands from superiors (Hoit; Rieckhoff, 2010). Above all, Rieckhoff, Hoit and Smith repeatedly challenge the film's authenticity and its realism with Rieckoff suggesting that the film should be regarded as a 'spectacular looking movie. But if you're looking for realism and how military relationships really work, I believe she [Kathryn Bigelow] missed the mark' (qtd. in Horn, Barnes and Parker, 2010). Smith took a particular issue with 'the portrayal of the EOD team as undisciplined, boozing, fighting children with no discipline or respect for the chain of command' (2010). Doubts about the film's realism came from an unlikely place when Jeremy Renner himself stated

There's no one really like the character of James... There was one guy that they all knew of and had heard about that would literally go up to an IED (Improvised Explosive Device) downrange and kick it. If it didn't go off, he won. There was that guy. But it's so uncommon that it's hard to connect. I'd break out the script and say 'here's a flaming car full of ordnance.' And they'd tell me everyone would run. The bomb techs and everyone would be out of there. Unless the president was in the UN building. That's the only reason – then your life becomes nothing. It's only realistic if there's someone of great importance inside the building.' (Qtd. in Massie, Mike and Joel n.d.s)

About this same topic Rieckhoff stated, 'We are not cowboys. We are not reckless. We are professionals. And a lot of the film would make you think the opposite' (qtd. in Horn, Barnes and Parker, 2010). Rieckhoff here raises a valid point concerning the affectual power popular cultural artefacts have on shaping how the public at large view cultural events: whether it is the wars in Iraq and Afghanistan as we have been exploring or other events like the assassination of John F. Kennedy in *JFK* (1991), the terrorist attacks on September 11 2001 in *World Trade Center* and *United 93*, the Watergate scandal in *All the President's Men* (1976), the 2004 Asian tsunami and earthquake in *The Impossible* (2012) and *Hereafter* (2010), or the civil war in Rwanda in *Hotel Rwanda* (2004). Sometimes these films can offer challenges to what we have described as the 'master narrative' which emerges as a shared consensus of understanding around any given event; as Alison Landsberg argued, they can 'enable individuals to have a personal connection to an event they did not live through, to see through another's eyes, they have the capacity to make possible alliances across racial, class and other chasms of difference' (2003: 156). However, as the vast majority of popular media emerge from capitalist, corporate owned enterprises, and in the specific case of the war film which is often directly supported by government organisations, the texts that are produced and disseminated most widely frequently adopt and therefore inculcate dominant ideological perspectives. Thus, the collective memories that are memorialised and culturally transmitted are not the progressive ones Landsberg describes, but rather reactionary ones which perpetuate the master narrative we have previously identified. In the case of *The Hurt Locker*, Rieckoff asserts that the public at large, with very minimal knowledge of the EOD, *what they do* and *how they do it*, might be very influenced by the portrayal of their actions in *The Hurt Locker*. This was something returned to by Richard Allen Smith who stated: 'Now, every person we encounter who hasn't served will think they understand us, because they happened to watch a work that is completely contrived fiction' (2010).

For those that criticised the film Boal had a specific answer, 'As I have said many times, the movie is not a documentary... We made creative decisions, and I hope people understand that those decisions were made respectfully and conscientiously' (qtd. in Bowman, 2010). His response is a valid one that he is entirely within his rights as an artist to express, just as it is the right of audiences, reviewers and scholars to categorically reject these assertions. We have seen how often those connected to the production of the film emphasised its authenticity, reportorial nature and its realism, and these claims had some very high-profile supporters: Defense Secretary M. Robert Gates described the film as 'authentic' adding that it was 'very compelling' (qtd. in Barnes, Parker and Horn, 2010) and Jim O'Neill, a veteran bomb disposal serviceman and head of the EOD Memorial Foundation, said, 'It kind of captures the whole environment over there' (qtd. in Bowman, 2010). Drew Sloan, veteran of two tours in Iraq and Afghanistan and Purple Heart medal recipient said, 'This is what's going on for the men and women who are fighting this war' (qtd. in Barnes, Parker and Horn, 2010). As the vast majority of viewers watching the film have not served with the military this places us in a rather difficult position. Where are we to stand on this matter? Are we to believe the likes of the veterans Hoit, Rieckhoff and Smith (2010) who state quite positively that the film is not to be regarded as authentic? Or the veterans Sloan, O'Neill and Defense Secretary M. Robert Gates who suggest that it is? Each seem equally emphatic in their assertions and each can point to moments in the film and their own experience to support their claims.

The film's final scenes in Iraq take place soon after James' double night time mission described in the previous chapter and begin with Eldridge being transported home out of the base on a chopper with his criticisms of James as quoted before. It is the last bomb mission in *The Hurt Locker* and the last time we will see Sanborn and James together. The sequence centres around what appears to be an Iraqi man placed in an explosive suicide vest against his will by insurgents. By then Sanborn and James seem to have come to some sort of understanding, but it is important to note that James *has not changed at all*, nor has he moderated his behaviour: he is the same rugged and uncompromising individualist he was the very first time we saw him during the first mission where he threw a smoke grenade to obscure himself from enemies without telling his team, where he confronted the taxi driver with his pistol, and where he pulled the daisy chain bomb out from the rubble of the streets. So, it seems that his earlier comments to Sanborn, 'You'll get it', which initially seemed arrogant and hubristic, have been proved right as Sanborn appears to have finally *got it*. If they did have some sort of alpha male power game, James has emerged as the winner: Sanborn asked him if he would ever be able to wear the bomb suit, to which James replied '*Hell no*' and while James' behaviour and attitude has been questioned in the film, it has been done so in a rather ambiguous fashion; it seems that the film has asked us to acknowledge that, as Richard Corliss did, that 'the army needs guys like James' (2008).

This final mission as the last 'in country' bomb sequence, is arguably one of the film's most important scenes and perhaps should be regarded as an encapsulation of its motifs, whatever they are. It is the dramatic climax of the film and one that offers deliberate parallels to the prologue, which featured the death of Thompson, with even many of its shots being framed in a similar way. Like the majority of the film it is impressively choreographed, artfully orchestrated and well performed by Jeremy Renner and Anthony Mackie. The Iraqi man (Suhail Aldabbebbach), who is not named in the film nor is he included in the credits, informs James through the translator that he has a family and pleads with the Americans to save him, begging them to remove the vest before it explodes. The translator informs James (and us the audience) that he should 'help this man... he's not a bad man' and James works hard to do so even when he realises that there is a timer which is ticking down from two minutes by the time James sees it, but we the audience do not. It is the only timer that the film about bomb disposal has given us, aside from the days on rotation which have reached just two remaining for this scene. James, as he has always been shown to do throughout the whole film, puts himself in great danger to save the man. Sanborn even tells him 'This is suicide man!', to which James replies, 'That's why they call it a suicide bomb right?' The previous scenes have asked us to question some of James' actions, if not his motives, which have always been good, but in his final bomb defusal he is reconsolidated into the film's mythic hero. The script says that James is like 'a moth to a flame, this is what he does' (2013: 103) and he continues to try to help the man as the clock timer ticks down, but the vest has been fastened with case hardened steel making his task impossible. Many who have written on this particular scene have persuasively argued that we should consider it as having metaphorical properties beyond that which are presented in the film's diegesis: Tasker says, 'In this sequence – and in the climactic scene in which a man pleads with James to defuse the bomb that he has been forced to wear – the bodies of Iraqi citizens are the territory over which the war is (inconclusively) waged' (2010: 63) and Guy Westwell writes, '*The Hurt Locker* is driven by a desire to convert the intractable political, ethnic, and religious conflicts that had come to define the war in Iraq into tangible, reducible, and solvable problems' (2013: 394). The scene does seem to encapsulate Boal's and Bigelow's attitude towards the broader parameters of the war which have remained implicit rather than explicit. James desperately tries to save the man, putting his life at great risk, but he simply cannot do it, as the man's fate has already been decided by the internecine fighting between Iraqis, who, as the film suggests, put such little value on human life compared to 'us' in the West. Like all the other scenes, we see the war through the prism of American experiences and the victim's fate functions more for what it is able to tell us about James rather than the man himself. Bigelow suggested that one of her aims for the film was that 'the hope is to be able to replicate the feel of war, the chaos of war, the messiness of war' and it is perhaps hard to deny that *The Hurt Locker* achieves this, but it is a certain kind of *chaos* and a certain kind of *messiness*, told from a very particular perspective. James leaves it until the very last seconds and apologises to the man before he leaves him – 'I can't get it off... I'm sorry' – then runs as fast as the bulky bomb suit allows him to away from the imminent explosion, just as Thompson did two hours of screen time before. As it was before, the explosion is repeated with multiple shots of extreme slow motion, only this time the EOD operative, William James, lives. With blood trickling down his nose, James pulls down his visor and we see what he sees, as we have throughout most of the film, a bright blue Iraqi sky with a solitary kite flying high above.

In the Humvee on the way back it is James who asks Sanborn, 'You alright?' and not the other way around. Sanborn admits to him 'I'm not ready to die' and expresses his intention to leave the EOD and his desire to have a son. The tone is a melancholy one and the non-diegetic music is present more than it has been in the film until now, as it appears the war has finally reached *Sanborn*, not, as one might expect, James, who was the one who was caught in the explosion and almost died. In this scene's final moments Sanborn asks James how he can do it, how he risks he life day after day after day, but James has no answer. All he can do is respond with a question of his own: 'Do *you* know why I am the way I am?' They are the last words the two characters say to each other and the film's final moments before it moves to America and takes James 'home'.

Figure 21

Figure 22

Figure 23

'With me, I think it's one…': Always 'in country', whether at home or abroad

After the end of the suicide bomb scene described above, James returns to the United States for a potent three-and-a-half minute-long sequence which concludes the film, apart from a brief coda. Even those critical of the film's depiction of the EOD unit in Iraq acknowledged that these final scenes with James at home with his wife and family offered a resonant and authentic depiction of the struggles that many veterans undergo returning to the domestic sphere after extended periods in combat. Paul Rieckhoff, who had said of *The Hurt Locker* that it 'tries to articulate that experience [of serving in Iraq], but those of us who have served in the military couldn't help but be distracted by a litany of inaccuracies that reveal not only a lack of research, but ultimately respect for the American military' (2010), commented that these scenes were persuasively realised and articulate. He wrote: 'One minute you are maneuvering your platoon through an ambush, the next you are maneuvering through the laundromat on the Lower East Side. It can be a challenging transition' (ibid.). *The Hurt Locker* does not show James in a laundromat, but instead in a supermarket in one of the film's most widely discussed moments. The transition between Baghdad and the US is itself an eloquent one which visually suggests that James may not be able to leave the war in Iraq and embrace life at home in America so easily. In the last image of Iraq we see a shot taken from inside the Humvee driving to the left with Iraqi children chasing alongside it which is match cut to a shot at about the same pace but this time of James, sometime later, pushing a shopping trolley in a supermarket with him reflected in the windows of refrigerator after refrigerator, each filled with a variety of food.

In the following scenes James is shown interacting with his partner, Connie (Evangeline Lilly) who he had telephoned earlier in the film from Iraq but had been unable to bring himself to talk to. Connie is the film's only female character, apart from one or two unnamed female Iraqis that the EOD unit is shown to interact with from time to time, but she is given barely a few lines of dialogue and only the faintest outline of a personality. In the supermarket she asks James 'You wanna go get us some cereal?', and then later at home 'You wanna chop those up for me?', handing him a bowl of carrots. Her screen time, as of those of the Iraqis throughout the film, is designed to reveal more about James than it is about her. Like the majority of war films, *The Hurt Locker* is a story about men and what men do, with women marginalised and relegated to the domestic sphere, largely ignoring the fact that by 2015 approximately fifteen percent of the US military was comprised of women (see Wood, n.d.s).[8]

James' return home is not portrayed as a refuge as one might expect, but a continuation of his personal and private war, and a trauma itself. He is shown playing with his infant son, clearing leaves from the gutters of his house, preparing food with his wife, staring at a static-filled television screen in an often used image which repeats frequently in the war film. The supermarket scene mentioned above offers a potent image of the emasculating potential of modern consumerist society as James is framed among the long aisles where he is confronted by literally hundreds of different varieties of cereal, paralysed by the surfeit of choice. The audience comes to realise that the pleasures of domesticity can never be enough for him: how can changing nappies and shopping for breakfast cereal compare to the adrenaline rush of bomb disposal? It is *there* among the bombs rather than *here* with his family that he feels most alive. Even the music playing in the scene accentuates this juxtaposition; rather than the heavy metal he has been associated with throughout his tour in Iraq, in the supermarket the store plays bland easy listening muzak, a style that, as Steve Waksman suggested, 'reinforces the sense that James is out of place in a seemingly normal setting; amidst the undemanding routine of everyday consumerism, he loses his bearings' (2011: 197). Like the majority of scenes in the film this one was interpreted very differently by a range of spectators: should it be considered a 'weak irony about life on the home front that a handful of Vietnam films conjured better a generation or two ago'? (Clover, 2009: 9), or a richly suggestive one pregnant with allusion and association to the mythological dimensions of masculinity and even to the Western genre itself, as Erik Dussere wrote: 'The idea is borrowed from the Western film tradition – the lone man who works to secure civilization and rule of law is himself unfit to live in the peaceful nation – and the film turns again to the supermarket as the spatial representation of a pervasively felt American emptiness by putting the cowboy in the cereal aisle' (2014: 31).

James' longest speech in the entire film comes shortly after the supermarket scene when he is putting his young son to bed. It is a scene which resonates for a variety of reasons not just because it is the most open he has been about his emotions and the honesty of his words, but

Figure 24

given that there is no-one to hear him apart from the small child, it is effectively a soliloquy. It also connects to a range of different moments throughout the film: from Sanborn's tearful admission that he wants a son, James' relationship with Beckham (alive and 'dead') and even the reluctant suicide bomber's translated words, which described him as being a 'family man'. In just a few minutes before the film's end credits it explains, in some ways, his drive and why it is that he does what he does. He says:

> You love playing with that. You love playing with all your stuffed animals. You love your Mommy, your Daddy. You love your pyjamas. You love everything, don't ya? Yeah. But you know what, buddy? As you get older... some of the things you love might not seem so special anymore. Like your Jack-in-a-Box. Maybe you'll realize it's just a piece of tin and a stuffed animal. And the older you get, the fewer things you really love. And by the time you get to my age, maybe it's only one or two things. With me, I think it's one...

Interestingly, these domestic scenes offer further connections to the real-life James, Jeffrey Sarver, the subject of Boal's 'The Man in the Bomb Suit'. Towards the end of Boal's article Sarver says, 'Not a day goes by that I don't think of my son' and that 'I know that I will not have the kind of relationship with him that my dad had with me' (2005: 152). Again, Sarver vocalises his love for his profession which is present in the film but, for the most part, left unsaid: 'Bagdhad was a blast' (2005: 153) and 'I need to get back to Iraq' (ibid.). In what is perhaps the closest either the article or the film come to the epigraph which begins the film taken from the work of Chris Hedges, he also says: 'Where else can I spend the morning taking apart an IED and in the afternoon drive down a road with 200 pounds of explosives in my truck, blowing up car bombs and trucks? I love all that stuff. Anything that goes boom. It's addictive' (ibid.). Boal's article does not inform readers whether Sarver redeployed, but his cinematic incarnation, William James, does. He recounts a story about Iraq to his wife which evokes both his own recent trip to the supermarket and the film's portrayal of Beckham: 'Some guy drove this truck to the middle of an Iraqi market. He starts passing out free candies, all the kids come running up, the families and stuff. He detonates... You know they need more bomb techs...' Once again violent acts are perpetrated by Iraqis on Iraqis, especially children, with Americans cast as the unambiguous saviours and the only barrier between Iraq and chaos. James cannot articulate this hunger to his wife and he volunteers for another tour of duty in Iraq, as many characters in war films which emerged from the war on terror era do (see *Stop-Loss*, *The Lucky Ones*, etc.).

Figure 25

As the film had offered an overlap between the transition from Iraq to America in its cut between the Humvee and the supermarket, it does something very similar for James' return, with the sounds of helicopter blades being heard in James' home before a cut to him 'in country' once again. Both transitions challenge the idea that even though there is a geographical divide between the two, the war does not end for veterans after they come home. The sounds of the helicopter blades are mixed with heavy metal music and as James exits the vehicle his purposeful stride is match cut with the stride continuing, only this time as he is dressed in full bomb suit back on the streets of Baghdad. At first the expression on his face is not entirely clear through the bomb suit's protective helmet and visor, *but it looks like a smile*. The script makes it clear that it is with the line 'A Middle-Eastern sun bathes James upturned face lengthening into a smile' (2013: 114) and also that 'James' face [is] glistening with pleasure' (ibid.). Are we to read this as a hero confidently striding towards his destiny, a 'mythicised evocation of men dedicated to their duty' (Tasker 2010: 58)? Or the arrogance of a man who will, sooner or later, come across a bomb that will kill him? It seems to be a deliberate allusion to the conclusion of John Ford's *The Searchers* (1956) where John Wayne's Ethan Edwards similarly walks away from domesticity to an uncertain future. Amy Taubin wrote:

> By dismantling close to 900 IEDs, James has saved who knows how many times that number of lives. And, as the film is careful to show, he's an equal opportunity savior. He's the latest and one of the most moving descendants of Ethan, *The Searchers*'s fissured icon of masculinity. Which in part is why the last shot of *The Hurt Locker*, an echo of Ethan turning his back on hearth and home and riding alone into the desert, breaks the heart. (2009: 35)

James cannot be himself at home: it is only on the frontier of Iraq that he is free to be the man he is away from the stultifying values of modern society and women and children. For James the daily countdown has begun again and the onscreen caption reads '365 DAYS IN ROTATION' as the cycle starts again.

A large number of films about the wars in Iraq and Afghanistan ended in similar ways to the conclusion of *The Hurt Locker*, by showing soldiers returning to the conflict, even after their own protestations that they would not or did not want to, as if there was something that drew them back. *American Sniper* concludes with Chris Kyle reluctantly turning his back on the war but helping veterans like himself who struggle to have an ordinary life after what they have experienced. It is one such veteran who murders Kyle in a scene which is not shown at the conclusion of Clint Eastwood's film, which itself evokes another John Wayne film, *The Shootist* (1976), before featuring extended images from Kyle's real-life funeral. This mythology is even more overt in Peter Berg's *Lone Survivor*, which concludes with a four-minute montage of images of the real-life soldiers as a cover version of David Bowie's "Heroes" is performed by Peter Gabriel. A few modern war films have dared to end not on moments of triumphant redemption and in doing so challenge it: *In the Valley of Elah* ends with Hank Deerfield (Tommy Lee Jones), the patriotic veteran of earlier American wars and the father of an Iraq veteran whom he discovers committed war crimes, turning the flag outside the local high school upside down in the classic signal of the country in distress and Brian De Palma's *Redacted* ends with one of its main characters being asked by his civilian friends for a war story, anticipating a tale of courage under fire, much like one offered by *The Hurt Locker* and *American Sniper*, but the tale he recounts to his friends is about the rape and murder of a fourteen year old Iraqi girl, one that proves impossible for them to process, so far is it disconnected from their understanding of the war. After an awkward silence they quickly change the subject and turn their heads away from him, just as James turned away from Beckham in *The Hurt Locker*.

Figure 26

Figure 27

References

8.   There are films about the wars in Iraq and Afghanistan which feature women in the service (see *Megan Leavey* [2017], *Camp X-Ray* [2014], and *Fort Bliss* [2014]) but they and their experiences are portrayed very differently to men in ways too complicated to explore here.

Conclusion

> *The Hurt Locker* leaves us with a narrative that blends fiction with empiricism, poetic license with documented realism, fallacy with truth, binaries that work to create its own cogent yet confusing arguments about war...
>
> David C. Ryan, 'The Psychology of a Narrative: *The Hurt Locker.*' *Identity Theory.* March 9 2010

I wish to conclude with a brief comparison between the categories Paul Storey identified as the defining characteristics of the Vietnam War film and *The Hurt Locker*, which we initially considered in Chapter One as both an indication of how far the films made about Vietnam influenced those made about Iraq and Afghanistan, but just as importantly how American films about the wars in which it participates tend to embody and perpetuate very similar ideas about itself regardless of the enemy it is fighting or the complicated nature of the geo-political conflicts themselves. As Storey points out, films depicting the Vietnam War are characterised by the following:

a) Their sustained disconnection from a political or historical understanding of the conflict being fought;

b) a committed disavowal of the extent of the US military advantage over the Vietnamese;

c) an absence of anti-war sentiment to the extent it was present at the time;

d) a predisposition towards forgetting Vietnamese casualties or an almost exclusive focus on American casualties;

e) Americanisation of narratives including the pronounced exclusion of Vietnamese who are constructed as an unambiguous Other;

f) atrocities committed are portrayed (which gives the appearance of the films being more challenging than they are) but presented as isolated acts of madness often brought about by the intense pressure soldiers are placed under;

g) the victimisation of the US soldier and by extension the US as a whole (2003: 107).

It is very clear to see that if one changes the word 'Vietnamese' to 'Iraqi' there are considerable similarities between his template and *The Hurt Locker*:

a) We have observed that Bigelow and Boal elect not to provide any sense of political or historical context to the conflict being fought, preferring instead the visceral immediacy of the restricted viewpoints of the EOD unit which are embraced both thematically and through a range of cinematic devices. In interviews they both suggested that this was to be regarded as a matter of authenticity and Realism, something which was often repeated by reviewers, but we have seen how it also might be interpreted as not as much of a withdrawal from ideology as some have suggested.

b) The film also perpetuates the idea of the US forces in Iraq as plucky, resilient and altruistic underdogs by focusing entirely on the underfunded EOD unit, negating the existence of $491 billion being spent in the conflict in 2004 alone, the year in which the film is set. It is the Americans who are constantly under threat, with not just *some* Iraqis framed as potential enemies but virtually every single individual they come across, even women and children. This too is rendered thematically and cinematically through the constant process of them being watched while at the same time making it seem entirely logical and appropriate that they view the world through their rifle sights.

c) Anti-war sentiment among both the soldiers and those at home is almost entirely erased from the narrative: we do witness one or two statements, as we have seen, both of which come from Eldridge but these are concerned primarily with the military's ability to fight the war appropriately. These few comments are far from the criticisms of the wars that were going on at home in the US and internationally. They also come from the man who is compromised by his inability to fight the war as it *needs* to be fought, unlike James and Sanborn, who express no doubts about what they are doing in Iraq at all.

d) When American soldiers die they are mourned by those within the diegesis and we audiences are clearly asked to grieve their loss. We are meant to understand these deaths as tragic, but those of Iraqis are portrayed in an entirely perfunctory way. This process highlights American heroism and nobility while at the same time as accentuating the cruelty and perfidy of the insurgents.

e) There is a pronounced lack of any meaningful characterisations of Iraqis a fact which is indicated, as we have seen, in how they are defined in the script and their descriptions (or lack of) in the credits. There is no mention or consideration of why the Americans might be meeting such vociferous contempt and aggression from the locals and no Iraqi is allowed to *ever* speak of their own experience. Furthermore, no Iraqi is allowed to suggest that they are *against* the American occupation apart from violent insurgents who are framed and coded throughout as terrorists. Thus, there is no legitimate opposition to the war afforded to Iraqis; if you are against the Americans being there then you are an insurgent/terrorist and, in many cases according to the film, an immoral monster.

f) The atrocities shown committed are by the Iraqi insurgents and they are, for the most part, invented by Bigelow and Boal. In particular this refers to the utilisation of the 'body bomb' and how it functions within the film and more broadly pertaining to the child in war trope. There are two examples of what might be seen as 'atrocities' against Iraqis but these are dealt with in a rather offhand fashion: Reed's order of the killing of an insurgent which happens off-screen and is something which might not even be registered by audiences during their first time watching, and the murder of the two captured and hooded Iraqis in the desert by the Ralph Fiennes character which, I would argue, is dealt with in a rather humorous way. These are not isolated acts of madness though, and their lives, as those of most Iraqis in the film with the exception of Beckham, are shown to be not worth grieving.

g) In what I would suggest to be the film's lasting and most resonant aspect, the primary victim of the war in Iraq as dramatised in *The Hurt Locker* is not the Iraqi population, thousands of whom were wounded or displaced, but the American soldier, whether he kills (*Brothers*, *Valley of Elah* and *Stop-Loss*) or even if he does not (*Jarhead* and *The Messenger*). We are asked to consider James as both the film's hero *and* its victim, for what he has sacrificed for the war, for his own country and for Iraq.

These creative decisions by Bigelow and Boal, as I have stated before, are entirely valid, and it cannot be doubted that the result is a film of exceptional skill and artistry by all those involved in its creation. One might suggest it is unfair to criticise one film for doing this, but when it is one of many and part of a whole genre, such argument is not just relevant but necessary. *The Hurt Locker*, like all films about America's conflicts made before, now or in the future is immersed in the ideological parameters of the culture which made them and to assert otherwise is questionable to say the least. We have explored the ambiguity at the heart of the film and challenged some of the assertions of the film-makers themselves. I would argue that the film has a cathartic function, as do many films of the genre, whether Boal or Bigelow intended it to or not, and it participates in the rewriting and re-remembering of the Iraq War as many films did for the Vietnam War in the years after it ended. The Iraq War as suggested by films like *The Hurt Locker*, *Lone Survivor* and *American Sniper* was a noble failure undertaken for the right reasons by men who did their best in impossible circumstances, but who paid a real price for it. James is perhaps emblematic of these men, but so is Chris Kyle, Marcus Lutrell and even Brandon King in *Stop-Loss*, Matt Ocre in *Sand Castle* and Billy Lynn in *Billy Lynn's Long Half-Time Walk*. They join the myriad of American soldiers in war films who sacrifice for their country and ask for little in return, who have been returned to in war film after war film throughout the decades. Yet to anyone with even a cursory knowledge of the conflict, the reasons for which it was embarked on and the way in which it was fought, this understanding emerges as highly problematic. The war film is a powerful and malleable genre in which an American sniper who shoots a child is brave and defensive, but an Iraqi one who, in his opinion, is fighting to protect his homeland, his religion and his family, is a despicable and evil coward, whose actions are evidence of their immorality, perfidy and godlessness. The documentarian and journalist John Pilger was very clear about why *The Hurt Locker* was so successful at the Academy Awards in an article entitled 'Why the Oscars are a con' (11 February 2010) when he wrote: 'This film offers a vicarious thrill through yet another standard-issue psychopath, high on violence in somebody else's country where the deaths of a million people are consigned to cinematic oblivion.' Even though Mark Boal might say that 'The movie is a two-hour-long argument that encapsulates all of our ideas about the conflict, the war and the people that are involved in it' (qtd. in Marshall, 2009: 202), but if it is an argument then it is a one-sided and rather superficial one which refuses to discuss the reasons the war was fought, offer any meaningful criticisms of *how* it was fought, or characterisations of any of those people the war was fought against or supposedly for.

Films about a nation's wars are dynamic cultural artefacts which can shape and even come to define the way a war is remembered for generations to come. For those of us who did not experience the Second World War and the Vietnam War our perceptions are defined by films about the conflict which *become* the war, regardless of their accuracy or authenticity. For the not so distant wars in Iraq and Afghanistan films like *The Hurt Locker*, *Lone Survivor* and *American Sniper* play vital roles in how they come to be understood in a cultural battleground which will be fought within the frames of American films as the years continue.

Filmography

12 Strong (Nicolai Fuglsig, 2018)

300 (Zack Snyder, 2006)

Act of Valour (Mike McCoy & Scott Waugh, 2012)

The Alamo (John Lee Hancock, 2004)

All the President's Men (Alan J. Pakula, 1976)

American Soldiers: A Day in Iraq (Sidney J. Furie, 2005)

American Sniper (Clint Eastwood, 2014)

Apocalypse Now (Francis Ford Coppola, 1979)

Avatar (James Cameron, 2009)

The Avengers (Joss Whedon, 2012)

Battle for Haditha (Nick Broomfield, 2007)

Billy Lynn's Long Half-Time Walk (Ang Lee, 2016)

Black Hawk Down (Ridley Scott, 2001)

Blanket Tossing a New Recruit (William Paley, 1898)

Bluestone 42 (BBC Three, 2013-2015)

Born on the Fourth of the July (Oliver Stone, 1989)

The Bourne Legacy (Tony Gilroy, 2012)

Brothers (Jim Sheridan, 2009)

Burial of the Maine Victims (William Paley, 1898)

Buffalo Soldiers (Gregor Jordan, 2003)

Captain Phillips (Paul Greengrass, 2013)

Casino Royale (Martin Campbell, 2005)

Casualties of War (Brian De Palma, 1989)

Children of Men (Alfonso Cuarón, 2004)

Close Encounters of the Third Kind (Steven Spielberg, 1977)

Coming Home (Hal Ashby, 1979)

Dear John (Lasse Hallström, 2010)

The Deer Hunter (Michael Cimino, 1978)

Dunkirk (Christopher Nolan, 2017)

E.T. the Extra-Terrestrial (Steven Spielberg, 1982)

First Blood (Ted Kotcheff, 1982)

Full Metal Jacket (Stanley Kubrick, 1987)

Fury (David Ayer, 2014)

Grace is Gone (James C. Strouse, 2007)

The Green Berets (Ray Kellog, 1968)

Green Zone (Paul Greengrass, 2010)

Hacksaw Ridge (Mel Gibson, 2016)

Heartbreak Ridge (Clint Eastwood, 1986)

Hearts and Minds (Peter Davis, 1974)

Hereafter (Clint Eastwood, 2010)

Home of the Brave (Irwin Winkler, 2006)

Homeland (Showtime, 2011-)

Hotel Rwanda (Terry George, 2004)

The Hurt Locker (Kathryn Bigelow, 2009)

The Impossible (J.A. Bayona, 2012)

In the Valley of Elah (Paul Haggis, 2008)

Iron Man (Jon Favreau, 2008)

Jarhead (Sam Mendes, 2005)

Jason Bourne (Paul Greengrass, 2016)

JFK (Oliver Stone, 1991)

The Kingdom (Peter Berg, 2007)

Kingdom of Heaven (Ridley Scott, 2005)

King Kong (Merian C. Cooper and Ernest B. Schoedsack, 1933)

L.A. Confidential (Curtis Hanson, 1997)

Life of Pi (Ang Lee, 2012)

Lions for Lambs (Robert Redford, 2007)

Logan (James Mangold, 2017)

Lone Survivor (Peter Berg, 2013)

The Lucky Ones (Neil Burger, 2008)

The Manchurian Candidate (John Frankenheimer, 1962)

Max (Boaz Yakin, 2014)

Megan Leavey (Gabriela Cowpwerthwaite, 2017)

The Messenger (Oren Moverman, 2009)

A Mighty Heart (Michael Winterbottom, 2007)

Mission: Impossible- Ghost Protocol (Brad Bird, 2011)

Pearl Harbour (Michael Bay, 2001)

Platoon (Oliver Stone, 1986)

Pulp Fiction (Quentin Tarantino, 1994)

Psycho (Alfred Hitchcock, 1960)

Raining Stones (Ken Loach, 1993)

Rambo: First Blood Part II (George P. Cosmatos, 1985)

Redacted (Brian De Palma, 2007)

Reign Over Me (Mike Binder, 2007)

Remember Me (Allen Coulter, 2010)

Rendition (Gavin Hood, 2007)

The Right Stuff (Philip Kaufman, 1983)

Riff Raff (Ken Loach, 1991)

Rules of Engagement (William Friedkin, 2000)

Sands of Iwo Jima (Allan Dwan, 1949)

Sand Castle (Fernando Coimbra, 2017)

Saving Private Ryan (Steven Spielberg, 1998)

The Searchers (John Ford, 1956)

The Shootist (Don Siegel, 1976)

Soldier Blue (Ralph Nelson, 1970)

Stop-Loss (Kimberly Peirce, 2008)

Syriana (Stephen Gaghan, 2005)

Taken (Pierre Morrel, 2008)

Team America: World Police (Trey Parker, 2004)

Top Gun (Tony Scott, 1986)

Tropic Thunder (Ben Stiller, 2008)

Troy (Wolfgang Peterson, 2004)

Ulzana's Raid (Robert Aldrich, 1972),

United 93 (Paul Greengrass, 2006)

The Wall (Doug Liman, 2017)

War of the Worlds (Steven Spielberg, 2005)

War Machine (David Michôd, 2017)

We Were Soldiers (Randall Wallace, 2002)

World Trade Center (Oliver Stone, 2006)

Zero Dark Thirty (Kathryn Bigelow, 2012)

Bibliography

Alpert, Robert. "*The Hurt Locker* Litigation: an adult's story." *Jump Cut*. No. 54, fall 2012 ←https://www.ejumpcut.org/archive/jc54.2012/alpertLawsuit/index.html→

Auster, Albert. (2005) 'Saving Private Ryan and American Triumphalism', in Robert T. Eberwein (ed.) *The War Film*. New Brunswick, NJ: Rutgers University Press, 205-213. Print.

Barkawi, Tarak. *Globalization and War*. Rowman and Littlefield, 2005. Print.

Barker, Martin. *A 'Toxic Genre': The Iraq War Films*. London: Pluto Press, 2011. Print.

Barnes, Julien E., Parker, Ned., Horn, John. "'The Hurt Locker' sets off conflict" *Los Angeles Times*. February 25 2010. ← http://articles.latimes.com/2010/feb/25/entertainment/la-et-hurt-locker26-2010feb26/2→

Barnett, Laura. "Another view on The Hurt Locker". *The Guardian*. 15 September 2009. https://www.theguardian.com/culture/2009/sep/15/the-hurt-locker-another-view

Bennett, Bruce and Diken, Bülent. "*The Hurt Locker*: Cinematic Addiction, 'Critique,' and the War on Terror." *Cultural Politics*. V.7 (n. 2). (2011) 165-188. Print.

Beevor, Antony. *The Second World War*. New York: Little, Brown, & Company, 2012. Print.

Boal, Mark. *Zero Dark Thirty The Shooting Script*. Newmarket Press: New York, 2013. Print.

----------"The Man in the Bomb Suit." *Playboy*. August/September 2005. 70-74, 148-153 https://cases.justia.com/federal/district-courts/california/cacdce/2:2010cv09034/488129/1/1.pdf

Bowman, Tom. "Veterans Say Exaggerations Abound In 'Hurt Locker'." March 5 2010. ← http://www.npr.org/templates/story/story.php?storyId=124319820→

Bradshaw, Peter. "The Hurt Locker." *The Guardian*. August 28 2009. ← https://www.theguardian.com/film/2009/aug/28/the-hurt-locker-review→

Brokaw, Tom. *The Greatest Generation*. New York: Random House, 1998. Print.

Burgoyne, Robert. "Embodiment in the war film: Paradise Now and *The Hurt Locker.*" *Journal of War & Culture Studies*, 5:1, (2012). 7-19. Print.

Burke, Jason. *The 9/11 Wars*. New York: Penguin, 2011. Print.

Butler, Judith. *Precarious Life: The Powers of Mourning and Violence*. London: Verso, 2004. Print.

Chantrill, Timothy. "What is the total U.S government spending?" https://www.usgovernmentspending.com/defense_spending (n.d.s)

Child, Ben. "CIA requested *Zero Dark Thirty* rewrites, memo reveals." *The Guardian*. 7 May 2013. Web, 3 Aug. 2013. ←http://www.guardian.co.uk/film/2013/may/07/zero-dark-thirty-cia-memo→.

Collin, Robbie. "Tom Hanks: Is this the most trusted man in America?" *The Telegraph*. 12 October 2013. http://www.telegraph.co.uk/culture/film/10373074/Tom-Hanks-Is-this-the-most-trusted-man-in-America.html?placement=CB2

Comolli, Jean-Louis, and Jean Narboni (1976) 'Cinema/Ideology/Criticism' in Bill Nichols (ed.) *Movies and Methods* (volume 1). Berkeley: University of California Press. 22-30. Originally printed in *Cahiers Du Cinema*. no. 216 October 1969. Print.

Clover, Joshua. "Allegory Bomb." *Film Quarterly* v.63 n.2 (2009): 8-9. Print.

Corliss, Richard. "The Hurt Locker: A Near-Perfect War Film." *Time*. 4 September 2008. ← http://content.time.com/time/arts/article/0,8599,1838615,00.html→

Creekmur, Corey. "The Sound of the 'War on Terror'." In J. Birkenstein, K. Randell and A. Froula, eds. *Reframing 9/11: Film, Popular Culture and the War on Terror* (New York & London: Continuum Press, 2010). 83-93. Print.

Crown, Sarah. "Brian Turner: Words Of War, 'Hurt Locker' Soldier Poet's New Book." *The Huffington Post*. 28 October 2010. http://www.huffingtonpost.com/2010/10/28/brian-turner-hurt-locker_n_775283.html

Daughtry, J. Martin. *Listening to War: Sound, Music, Trauma and Survival in Wartime Iraq*. Oxford: Oxford University Press, 2015. Print.

Dawson, Nick. "Time's Up." In *Kathryn Bigelow Interviews*. Ed. Peter Keough. Jackson: University of Mississippi Press, 2013. 142-149. Print.

Denby, David. "Anxiety Tests." *The New Yorker*. 29 June 2009. Web. 30 Jan. 2010. ←http://www.newyorker.com/arts/critics/cinema/2009/06/29/090629crci_cinema_denby?currentPage=all→.

Diken, Bülent. *Revolt, Revolution, Critique: The Paradox of Society*. London: Routledge, 2012. Print.

Dussere, Erik. *America Is Elsewhere: The Noir Tradition in the Age of Consumer Culture*. New York: Oxford University Press, 2014. Print.

Edelstein, David. "Explosive Material." 22 June 2009. *New York Magazine*. ← http://nymag.com/movies/reviews/57462/→

Elfman, Malin. "Interview with Jeremy Renner for The Hurt Locker." Screencrave. June 22, 2009. ← http://www.jeremyleerenner.com/12-articles/203-june-22-2009-interview-with-jeremy-renner-for-the-hurt-locker-screencrave-com→

Everheart, Bill. "Summer comes earlier to movie season." *The Berkshire Eagle*. May 1 2009. ← http://www.berkshireeagle.com/stories/summer-comes-earlier-to-movie-season,216397→

"August 2009 -- Exclusive 'The Hurt Locker' Interview with Star Jeremy Renner (gonewiththetwins.com)" The Massie Twins. https://www.jeremyleerenner.com/12-articles/196-august-2009-exclusive-the-hurt-locker-interview-with-star-jeremy-renner-gonewiththetwins-com

Fiske, John. *Television Culture* (Second Edition). Abingsdon: Routledge, 2011. Print.

Fleming Jr., Mike. "American Sniper's Bradley Cooper On Less Is More, And Other Lessons Learned From Eastwood, De Niro And David O' *Deadline*. February 11 2015. ← http://deadline.com/2015/02/american-sniper-bradley-cooper-finding-truth-eastwood-de-niro-and-david-o-russell-1201371278/→

Forché, Carolyn. http://www.brianturner.org/poetry/ (n.d.s)

Foundas, Scott. "The Hurt Locker, Ticking Time Bomb of a Movie." *The Village Voice*. June 24, 2009. ← https://www.villagevoice.com/2009/06/24/

the-hurt-locker-ticking-time-bomb-of-a-movie/→

Goff, Stan. *Full Spectrum Disorder: The Military in the New American Century*. Brooklyn, NJ: Soft Skull Press, 2004. Print.

Greenstock, Jeremy. *Iraq: The Cost of War*. London: William Heinnman, 2017. Print.

Grove, Martin A. "A sound policy for 'The Hurt Locker'" *The Hollywood Reporter*. 18 February 2010. ← http://www.hollywoodreporter.com/news/sound-policy-hurt-locker-20847→

Hedges, Chris. *War Is a Force That Gives Us Meaning*. New York: Public Affairs, 2002. Print.

Hemmeter, Thomas. "Hitchcock's Narrative Modernism: Ironies of Fictional Time." In *A Companion to Alfred Hitchcock*. Eds. Thomas Leitch and Leland Poague. Malden: Wiley Blackwell, 2011. 67-84. Print.

Hinds, Julie "Army bomb expert claims 'Hurt Locker' based on him." *USA Today*. March 3, 2010. http://usatoday30.usatoday.com/life/movies/news/2010-03-03-hurt-locker-lawsuit_N.html)

Hoad, Phil. "The best battle scenes ever shot from *Apocalypse Now* to *Hacksaw Ridge*." *The Guardian*. 26 January 2017. ← https://www.theguardian.com/film/2017/jan/26/the-best-battle-scenes-ever-shot-from-apocalypse-now-to-hacksaw-ridge→.

Hoit, Kate. "The Hurt Locker Doesn't Get This Vet's Vote." *The Huffington Post*. 6 April 2010. ← http://www.huffingtonpost.com/kate-hoit/the-hurt-locker-doesnt-ge_b_449043.html→

Holderness, Graham. *Tales From Shakespeare: Creative Collisions*. Cambridge: Cambridge University Press, 2014. Print.

Hond, Paul. "Shoot Shoot, Bang Bang." In *Kathryn Bigelow Interviews*. Ed. Peter Keough. Jackson: University of Mississippi Press, 2013. 203-211. Print.

Horn, John, Barnes, Julian E. Parker, Ned. "'The Hurt Locker' sets off conflict within military." February 26 2010. ← http://www.seattletimes.com/nation-world/the-hurt-locker-sets-off-conflict-within-military/→

Horton, Robert. "An Interview with *Hurt Locker*'s Kathryn Bigelow." In *Kathryn Bigelow Interviews*. Ed. Peter Keough. Jackson: University of Mississippi Press, 2013. 150-152. Print.

Hoskins, Andrew. *Televising War: From Vietnam to Iraq*. London: Continuum, 2004. Print.

"*The Hurt Locker* Production Notes" N.A.S. 13 September 2014. ←http:// madeinatlantis.com/movies_central/2009/hurt_locker_production_details. htm→

"Iraq Most Wanted Fast Facts". *CNN*. 9 March 2017. ←http://edition.cnn. com/2013/10/30/world/meast/iraq-most-wanted-fast-facts/index.html→

Jeansonne, Glen and Luhrssen, David. *War on the Silver Screen. Shaping America's Perception of History*. Lincoln, Nebraska: Potomac Books, 2014. Print.

Jeffords, Susan. *Hard Bodies: Hollywood Masculinity in the Reagan Era*. New Brunswick, NJ: Rutgers University Press, 1994. Print.

Jeffrey S. Sarver v. The Hurt Locker LLC et al, UNITED STATES DISTRICT COURT DISTRICT OF NEW JERSEY ← https://cases.justia.com/ federal/district-courts/california/cacdce/2:2010cv09034/488129/1/0. pdf?ts=1376357354→

Jenkins, Tricia. *The CIA in Hollywood. How the Agency Shapes Film and Television*. Austin: University of Texas Press, 2012. Print.

Katovsky, Bill and Carlson, Timothy. *The Media at War in Iraq*. The Lyons Press, 2003. Print.

Kavadlo, Jessie. *American Popular Culture in the Era of Terror: Falling Skies, Dark Knights Rising, and Collapsing Cultures*. Santa Barbara, California: Praeger, 2015. Print.

Keegan, John. *The Second World War*. London: Pimlico Press, 1989. Print.

Kellner, Douglas. *Media Culture: Cultural Studies, Identity and Politics between the Modern and the Postmodern*. New York: Routledge, 1995.

Kolker, Robert. *A Cinema of Loneliness*. Oxford: Oxford University Press, 2011. Print.

Koppl, Rudy. 'The Hurt Locker. Blurring the Lines Between Sound and Score.' (n.d.s) Music From the Movies. ←http://www.musicfromthemovies. com/index5.php?option=com_content&view=article&id=%27%20.%20 (63)%20.%20%27ottosson→

Landsberg, Alison. "Prosthetic Memory: Total Recall and Blade Runner." Cyberspace/Cyberbodies/Cyberpunk: Cultures of Technological Embodiment. Eds. Mike Featherstone and Roger Burrows. London: Sage, 1995. 175-190. Print.

----------. "Prosthetic memory: the ethics and politics of memory in an age of mass culture." Memory and Popular Film. Ed. Paul Grainger. Manchester: Manchester University Press, 2003. 144-161. Print.

Maas, Peter. "Don't Trust Zero Dark Thirty." The Atlantic. 13 Dec. 2012. Web. 4 Aug. 2013. ←http://www.theatlantic.com/entertainment/ archive/2012/12/dont-trust-zero-dark-thirty/266253/→.

Marshall, Kingsley. "The Hurt Locker Interview: Kathryn Bigelow and Mark Boal." In Kathryn Bigelow Interviews. Ed. Peter Keough. Jackson: University of Mississippi Press, 2013. 199-202. Print.

Markert, John. Post-9/11 Cinema: Through a Lens Darkly. Lanham, Maryland: The Scarecrow Press, Inc., 2011. Print.

Massey, Mike and Massie, Joel. "Interview: Jeremy Renner from "The Hurt Locker"". n.d.s http://gonewiththetwins.com/new/interview-jeremy-renner-hurt-locker/

McSweeney, Terence. The 'War on Terror' and American Film: 9/11 Frames Per Second. Edinburgh: Edinburgh University Press, 2014. Print.

Mirrlees, Tanner, Global Entertainment Media: Between Cultural Imperialism and Cultural Globalization. New York: Routledge, 2013. Print.

Mondello, Bob. "'Hurt Locker': An Explosive Look At The Iraq War." NPR. June 26 2009. ← http://www.npr.org/templates/story/story. php?storyId=105755842→

Nathan, Ian. "The Hurt Locker Review." Empire. July 29 2009. ← http:// www.empireonline.com/movies/hurt-locker/review/→

Nochimson, Martha. P., "Kathryn Bigelow: Feminist pioneer or tough guy in drag?" *Salon.* February 25 2010. ← http://www.salon.com/2010/02/24/bigelow_3/→

Noonan, Peggy. "Welcome Back, Duke From the ashes of Sept. 11 arise the manly virtues." *Wall Street Journal.* 12 Oct. 2001. Web. 12 May 2012. ←http://online.wsj.com/article/SB122451174798650085.html→.

----------. "The Right Man." *The Washington Post.* 30 Jan. 2003. Web. 29 May 2012. ←http://online.wsj.com/article/SB1043895876926710064.html→.

O'Brien, Wesley. *Music in American Combat Films: A Critical Study.* McFarland and Company, 2012. Print.

Peebles, Stacey. *Welcome to the Suck: Narrating the American Soldier's Experience in Iraq.* Ithaca and London: Cornell University Press, 2011. Print.

Pendleton, David. "A Discussion with Kathryn Bigelow at the Harvard Film Archive." In *Kathryn Bigelow Interviews.* Ed. Peter Keough. Jackson: University of Mississippi Press, 2013. 180-195. Print.

Pheasant-Kelly, Francis. *Fantasy Film Post 9/11.* New York: Palgrave MacMillan, 2013.

King, Geoff. *Spectacular Narratives: Hollywood in the Age of the blockbuster.* London: I B Tauris & Co, 2000. Print.

Pilger, John. ""Why the Oscars are a con". *The New Statesman.* 11 February 2010. http://www.newstatesman.com/film/2010/02/pilger-iraq-oscar-american-war

Polan, Dana. 'Movies, a Nation, and New Identities' in Timothy Corrigan (ed.) *American Cinema of the 2000s: Themes and Variations.* New Brunswick: Rutgers University Press, 2012. 216-238. Print.

Purse, Lisa. *Contemporary Action Cinema.* Edinburgh: Edinburgh University Press, 2011. Print.

Rainer, Peter. "Review: 'The Hurt Locker'" June 26 2009. *Christian Science Monitor.* http://www.csmonitor.com/The-Culture/Movies/2009/0626/p17s07-almo.html

Rieckhoff, Tom. "Veterans: Why 'The Hurt Locker' Isn't Reality."
Newsweek. 23 February 2010. ← newsweek.com/veterans-why-hurt-locker-isnt-reality-75205→

Robb, David L. *Operation Hollywood: How the Pentagon Shapes and Censors the Movies*. New York: Prometheus Books, 2004. Print.

Robinson, Janet. S., "The gendered Geometry of War in Kathryn Bigelow's *The Hurt Locker* (2008)." In eds. Karen A. Ritzenhoff and Jakub Kazecki. *Heroism and Gender in War Films*. New York: Palgrave Macmillan, 2014. 153-172. Print.

Rubin, Steven Jay. *Combat Films: American Realism, 1945-2010* (Second Edition). Jefferson, NC: McFarland & Company, Inc., 2011. Print.

Ryan, David C. "The Psychology of a Narrative: The Hurt Locker." *Identity Theory*. March 9 2010. ← http://www.identitytheory.com/the-psychology-of-a-narrative-the-hurt-locker/→

Schwarzbaum, Lisa. "*The Hurt Locker*." *Entertainment Weekly*. June 17 2009. ← http://ew.com/article/2009/06/17/hurt-locker-2/→

Scott, A.O. "Apolitics and the War Film." *New York Times* 6 Feb 2010. http://www.nytimes.com/2010/02/07/weekinreview/07aoscott.html?_r=0

Selbo, Jule. *Film Genre for the Screenwriter*. New York: Routledge, 2015. Print.

Smith, Richard Allen. "The Hurt Locker: Inaccurate and Disrespectful." *The Huffington Post*. June 8 2010. ← http://www.huffingtonpost.com/richard-allen-smith/the-hurt-lockeri-inaccura_b_489976.html→

Smith, M. "A World of 'Hurt': War is a Drug, The Hurt Locker Reminds Us." *Tulsa World*. July 31 2009. ←http://www.tulsaworld.com/scene→

Steritt, David. "Screening the politics out of the Iraq War." *Counter Punch*. 24 July 2009. ← http://www.counterpunch.org/2009/07/24/screening-the-politics-out-of-the-iraq-war/→

Storey, John. "The articulation of memory and desire: from Vietnam to the war in the Persian Gulf." *Memory and Popular Film*. Ed. Paul Grainge. Manchester: Manchester University Press, 2003. Print.

Sturken, Marita. *Tangled Memories: The Vietnam War, the AIDS Epidemic, and the Politics of Remembering*. Los Angeles and London: University of California Press, 1997. Print.

Suid, Lawrence H. *Guts & Glory: The Making of the American Military Image in Film*. Lexington, KY: The University Press of Kentucky, 2002. Print.

Tasker, Yvonne and Atakav, Eylem. "The Hurt Locker: Male Intimacy, Violence and the Iraq War Movie". *Sinicine*, v.7 n.2. 2010: 57-70. Print.

Taubin, Amy. "Hard Wired." *Film Comment* v.45 n.3. (2009): 30-32, 34-35. Print.

Taylor, A. J. P. *The Origins of the Second World War*. London: Hamish Hamilton, 1961. Print.

Terkel, Studs. *"The Good War": An Oral History of World War II*. New York: Pantheon Books, 1984.

Thomson, David. *The Cinema of Eisenstein*. London: Routledge, 2005. Print.

Tobias, Scott. "Interview: Kathryn Bigelow." In *Kathryn Bigelow Interviews*. Ed. Peter Keough. Jackson: University of Mississippi Press, 2013. 153-158. Print.

DuToit, Kim. "The Pussification Of The Western Male." Web. 22 June 2013. ←http://talltown.us/guns/nancyboys.htm→.

Trafton, John. *The American Civil War and the Hollywood War Film*. Basingstoke: Palgrave Macmillan, 2016. Print.

Turan, Kenneth. Review. *Los Angeles Times*. June 26 2009. http://articles. latimes.com/2009/jun/26/entertainment/et-hurtlocker26

Turner, Brian. *Here, Bullet*. Farmington, Maine: Alice James Books, 2005. Print.

Van Munster, Rens. "Inside War: Counterinsurgency and the Visualisation of Violence" in Rens Van Munster and Casper Sylvest (ed.) *Documenting World Politics: A Critical Companion to IR and Non-Fiction Film*. London and New York: Routledge, 2015: 114-132. Print.

"VETERANS: WHY 'THE HURT LOCKER' ISN'T REALITY". *Newsweek.* Newsweek Staff. 23 February 2010. ←http://www.newsweek.com/veterans-why-hurt-locker-isnt-reality-75205→

"Waiting for John Wayne." N.A.S. *The Economist.* August 28 2008. ← http://www.economist.com/node/12000929→

Waksman, Steve. "War is Heavy Metal: Soundtracking the US War in Iraq." In *The Politics of Post 9/11 Music: Sound, Trauma, and the Music Industry in the Time of Terror.* Eds. Joseph P. Fisher and Brian Flota. New York: Routledge, 2011. 185-204. Print.

Walls, Seth Colter. "The Hollowness of The Hurt Locker." *Newsweek.* 21 January 2010. ← http://www.newsweek.com/hollowness-hurt-locker-71021→

Weintraub, Steve. "Director Kathryn Bigelow and Screenwriter Mark Boal Interview THE HURT LOCKER" June 7 2009. http://collider.com/director-kathryn-bigelow-and-screenwriter-mark-boal-interview-the-hurt-locker/

Weitzmann, Elizabeth. "'The Hurt Locker': Iraq war thriller is explosive drama." *New York Daily News.* 25 June 2009. ← http://www.nydailynews.com/entertainment/movies/hurt-locker-iraq-war-thriller-explosive-drama-article-1.170514→

Westwell, Guy. *War Cinema: Hollywood on the Front Line.* London: Wallflower Press, 2006. Print.

----------"In Country: Narrating the Iraq War in Contemporary US Cinema." In *A Companion to the Historical Film.* Ed. Robert Rosenstone and Constantin Parveluscu. Chichester, John Wiley & Sons, 2013. 384-407. Print.

----------. *Parallel Lines: Post-9/11 American Cinema.* London: Wallflower Press, 2014. Print

Whitsitt, Sam. ""Come Back to the Humvee Ag'in Will Honey," or a few comments about the sexual politics of Kathryn Bigelow's The Hurt Locker." *Jump Cut: A Review of Contemporary Media.* No. 52, summer 2010. https://www.ejumpcut.org/archive/jc52.2010/whitsittHurtLocker/text.html

Wills, Gary. *John Wayne's America: The Politics of Celebrity.* London: Faber and Faber, 1997. Print.

Wood, Jenny n.d.s. "A History of Women in the US. Military". https://www.infoplease.com/us/military-affairs/history-women-us-military

Woodall, Bernie. "US. bomb expert says 'Hurt Locker' stole his story", March 4 2010. http://www.reuters.com/article/us-hurtlocker-lawsuit-idUSTRE6220HO20100304

Young, Marilyn. *The Vietnam Wars 1945-1990.* New York: Harper Collins, 1991. Print.

---------- "*The Hurt Locker*: War as a Video Game." *Perspectives on History.* November 2009. https://www.historians.org/publications-and-directories/perspectives-on-history/november-2009/the-hurt-locker-war-as-a-video-game

----------------. "On 9/11, New Yorkers Faced the Fire in the Minds of Men." *The Guardian.* 11 Sept. 2006. 30. Print.

Žižek, Slavoj. "Green Berets with a Human Face." *New Statesman*, 23 March 2010. Web. 22 July 2011. ←http://www.egs.edu/faculty/slavoj-zizek/articles/green-berets-with-a-human-face/→.

ALSO
AVAILABLE

Studying Waltz with Bashir
Giulia Miller

Studying Ida
Sheila Skaff